First World War
and Army of Occupation
War Diary
France, Belgium and Germany

25 DIVISION
75 Infantry Brigade
Worcestershire Regiment
1/8th Battalion
1 September 1918 - 28 February 1919

WO95/2251/2

The Naval & Military Press Ltd
www.nmarchive.com
Published in association with The National Archives

Published by

The Naval & Military Press Ltd

Unit 10 Ridgewood Industrial Park,

Uckfield, East Sussex,

TN22 5QE England

Tel: +44 (0) 1825 749494

www.naval-military-press.com

www.nmarchive.com

This diary has been reprinted in facsimile from the original. Any imperfections are inevitably reproduced and the quality may fall short of modern type and cartographic standards.

© Crown Copyright
Images reproduced by permission of The National Archives, London, England, 2015.

Contents

Document type	Place/Title	Date From	Date To
Heading	WO95/2251-2		
Heading	25th Division 75th Infy Bde 1-8th Bn Worcester Regt Sep 1918-Feb 1919 (From 48 Div. 144 Bde Italy) and (1915 Apr-1917. Oct France same Div & Bde)		
War Diary	Asiago Plateau Rt Front Rt Bde Club Camp	01/09/1918	09/09/1918
War Diary	Rt Front Rt Bde	10/09/1918	11/09/1918
War Diary	Centrale	12/09/1918	13/09/1918
War Diary	Train	14/09/1918	15/09/1918
War Diary	France St Rigquier	16/09/1918	17/09/1918
War Diary	Agenvillers	18/09/1918	26/09/1918
War Diary	Warloy	27/09/1918	28/09/1918
War Diary	Montauban	29/09/1918	30/09/1918
War Diary	Combles	01/10/1918	01/10/1918
War Diary	Nurlu	02/10/1918	02/10/1918
War Diary	St Emile	03/10/1918	04/10/1918
War Diary	Beaurevoir	05/10/1918	07/10/1918
War Diary	Ponchaux	08/10/1918	09/10/1918
War Diary	Honnechy	09/10/1918	11/10/1918
War Diary	Serain	12/10/1918	15/10/1918
War Diary	Honnechy	16/10/1918	17/10/1918
War Diary	Honnechy (sunhen Road)	17/10/1918	18/10/1918
War Diary	St Benin	19/10/1918	19/10/1918
War Diary	Basuel	20/10/1918	20/10/1918
War Diary	St Benin	21/10/1918	22/10/1918
War Diary	Eveque Wood	23/10/1918	23/10/1918
War Diary	Fontaine	24/10/1918	24/10/1918
War Diary	Pommereuil	25/10/1918	31/10/1918
Miscellaneous	1/8 Bn The Worcestershire Regt. Narrative Of Operations	05/10/1918	05/10/1918
Operation(al) Order(s)	1/8th Bn. The Worcestershire Regt. Operation Order No. 87	01/10/1918	01/10/1918
Operation(al) Order(s)	1/8th Bn. The Worcestershire Regt. Operation Order No. 88	02/10/1918	02/10/1918
Operation(al) Order(s)	1/8th Bn. The Worcestershire Regt. Operation Order No. 89	03/10/1918	03/10/1918
Operation(al) Order(s)	1/8th Bn Worcestershire Regt. Operation Order No. 90	04/10/1918	04/10/1918
Operation(al) Order(s)	1/8th Bn The Worcestershire Rgt. Operation Order No. 91	05/10/1918	05/10/1918
War Diary	1/8th Bn The Worcestershire Regt. Operation Order No. 92	09/10/1918	09/10/1918
Miscellaneous	1/8th Bn The Worcestershire Regt. Narrative Of Operation.	09/10/1918	09/10/1918
Operation(al) Order(s)	1/8th Bn The Worcestershire Regt. Operation Order No. 93	10/10/1918	10/10/1918
Operation(al) Order(s)	1/8th Bn The Worcestershire Regt. Operation Order No.94	11/10/1918	11/10/1918
Operation(al) Order(s)	1/8 Bn The Worcestershire Regt. Operation Order No. 95	16/10/1918	16/10/1918
Operation(al) Order(s)	1/8 Bn The Worcestershire Regt. Operation Order No. 96	17/10/1918	17/10/1918

Type	Description	Date From	Date To
Operation(al) Order(s)	1/8 Bn The Worcestershire Regt. Operation Order No. 97	18/10/1918	18/10/1918
Miscellaneous	1/8 Bn The Worcestershire Regt. Narrative Of Operations.	18/10/1918	18/10/1918
Diagram etc	Dispositions 1/8 Bn Worcestershire Rgt	18/10/1918	18/10/1918
Operation(al) Order(s)	1/8 Bn The Worcestershire Rgt. Operation Order No. 98	20/10/1918	20/10/1918
Miscellaneous	Amendment to O.O. 99	22/10/1918	22/10/1918
Miscellaneous	Addendum to O.O. 99	22/10/1918	22/10/1918
Operation(al) Order(s)	1/8th Bn The Worcestershire Regt. Operation Order No. 99 App (Q)	22/10/1918	22/10/1918
Miscellaneous	App (R)	23/10/1918	23/10/1918
Miscellaneous	1/8th Bn Worcestershire Rgt. App (S)	24/10/1918	24/10/1918
Operation(al) Order(s)	1/8 Bn. The Worcestershire Regt. Operation Order No. 100 Appendix T	24/10/1918	24/10/1918
Operation(al) Order(s)	1/8 Bn The Worcestershire Rgt Operation Order No. 101 App U	24/10/1918	24/10/1918
Miscellaneous	75 Infantry Brigade App V	26/10/1918	26/10/1918
Miscellaneous	1/8 Bn The Worcestershire Regt. App W		
War Diary	Pommereuil	01/11/1918	02/11/1918
War Diary	Landrecies	03/11/1918	04/11/1918
War Diary	Maroilles	05/11/1918	06/11/1918
War Diary	Marbaix	07/11/1918	07/11/1918
War Diary	Preux	08/11/1918	13/11/1918
War Diary	Le Cateau	14/11/1918	28/11/1918
War Diary	Carnieres	29/10/1918	30/10/1918
Operation(al) Order(s)	1/8th Bn The Worcestershire Regt. Operation Order No. 102	01/11/1918	01/11/1918
Miscellaneous	1/8th Bn The Worcestershire Regt Instructions No. 1	02/11/1918	02/11/1918
Operation(al) Order(s)	1/8th Bn The Worcestershire Regt. Operation Order No. 103	03/11/1918	03/11/1918
Operation(al) Order(s)	1/8th Bn The Worcestershire Regt. Operation Order No. 104	03/11/1918	03/11/1918
Miscellaneous	1/8th Bn. The Worcestershire Regt.		
Miscellaneous	1/8th Bn The Worcestershire Regiment. Narrative of Operations	06/11/1918	06/11/1918
Operation(al) Order(s)	1/8 Bn The Worcestershire Regt. Operation Order No. 105	05/11/1918	05/11/1918
Operation(al) Order(s)	1/8 Bn The Worcestershire Regt. Operation Order No. 106	05/11/1918	05/11/1918
Operation(al) Order(s)	1/8 Bn The Worcestershire Regt. Operation Order No. 107	07/11/1918	07/11/1918
Operation(al) Order(s)	1/8 Bn The Worcestershire Regt. Operation Order No. 108	08/11/1918	08/11/1918
Operation(al) Order(s)	1/8 Bn The Worcestershire Regt. Operation Order No. 109	13/11/1918	13/11/1918
Operation(al) Order(s)	1/8 Bn The Worcestershire Regt. Operation Order No. 110	17/11/1918	17/11/1918
Operation(al) Order(s)	1/8th Bn. The Worcestershire Regiment. Operation Order No. 111	28/11/1918	28/11/1918
Miscellaneous	25th Division "G"	14/11/1918	14/11/1918
War Diary	Carnieres	01/12/1918	15/12/1918
War Diary	Cambrai	16/12/1918	28/02/1919

620 95/2251/2

25TH DIVISION
75TH INFY BDE

1-8TH BN WORCESTER REGT

SEP 1918 - FEB 1919

(FROM 48 DIV. 144 Bde ITALY)

and
1915 APR — 1917 OCT France same DIV + BDE

Copy of Original SP 16 Feb 19

Copy List

WAR DIARY
or
INTELLIGENCE SUMMARY
(Erase heading not required.)

1/8th Bn. The Worcestershire Regt.

Army Form C. 2118.

95/75

M 42

Place	Date	Hour	Summary of Events and Information	Remarks and references to Appendices
BESIEGED PLOTEAU	N Bar Alt Rlw Sept 1st 1918	1	Day guards. Bn employed improving trenches.	31 y 6
CLUB CAMP GRAMEZZA		2	Bn relieved by 1st Royal Berks proceeded to CLUB CAMP near GRAMEZZA	31 y 6
		3	Coy at disposal of Coy Commanders for inspection of baths.	31 y 6
		4	Training according to Programme of training drawn up by Commander. A & D Coy Platoon Scheme; B Coy Assault Course; R Coy Compass Marching	31 y 6
		5	Programme of training — A Coy Assault Course; B Coy Platoon Scheme; C Coy Range; D Coy Compass Marching	31 y 6
		6	Programme of training. A Coy Compass Marching; B Coy Company Scheme; C Coy Platoon Scheme; D Coy Assault Course.	31 y 6
		7	Programme of training — A Coy Range; B Coy Compass Marching; C Coy Assault Course; D Coy Company Scheme.	31 y 6
		8	Bn carried out a tactical exercise (Bn in attack)	31 y 6
		9	Inspection of billets by G.O.C. Division.	31 y 6
Mt Suffat Left Bde		10	Bn relieved 1/8 R Warwickshire Regt in Rt Support position. Left Bde	31 y 6
		11	Bn employed improving trenches.	31 y 6

42.1

Copy of Original.

Army Form C. 2118.

WAR DIARY
INTELLIGENCE SUMMARY. 1/8th Bn. The Worcestershire Regt.

(Erase heading not required.)

Instructions regarding War Diaries and Intelligence Summaries are contained in F. S. Regs., Part II. and the Staff Manual respectively. Title pages will be prepared in manuscript.

Place	Date 1918 Sept	Hour	Summary of Events and Information	Remarks and references to Appendices
CENTRALE	12		Bn proceeded by motor lorries to camp at CENTRALE.	A-Y 16
	13		Coys at disposal of Coy Commanders	A-Y 16
TRAIN	14		Bn entrained for FRANCE at THIENE — to Bn HQ, A+D Coys ent # #1 pm,	A-Y 16
	15		remainder at 8.41 am	A-Y 16
			Train	A-Y 16
	16		Train	A-Y 16
FRANCE ST RIQUIER	17		Bn detrained at ST RIQUIER. 1st Train 5 pm; 2nd Train 10.30 pm and marched to ACHEUX VILLERS. Bn became part of 75th Bde, 25th Division.	A-Y 16
ACHEUX VILLERS	18		Coys at disposal of Coy Commanders.	A-Y 16
	19		Coys reorganized into 4 Plns, each pln 3 sections (2 rifle sections + 1 double L.G. section). The establishment of Lewis Guns was increased to 32.	A-Y 16
			A Lewis Gun section was also established at Bn HQ with 4 L.G.'s for Anti-Aircraft work.	A-Y 16
	20		Training according to Training scheme. Training of extra L.Gs commenced.	A-Y 16
	21		Inspection by Brig. Gen. RICHARDSON.	A-Y 16
	22		Voluntary Church Service and Baths.	A-Y 16

Copy of Original.

Army Form C. 2118.

WAR DIARY
or
INTELLIGENCE SUMMARY. 1/8th Bn. The Worcestershire Regt.
(Erase heading not required.)

Instructions regarding War Diaries and Intelligence Summaries are contained in F. S. Regs., Part II. and the Staff Manual respectively. Title pages will be prepared in manuscript.

Place	Date 1918 Sept	Hour	Summary of Events and Information	Remarks and references to Appendices
ACHEVILLERS	23rd		Training according to Training Scheme & Baths.	JYB
	24		Coys. have Demo. Business regarding as disposal of Coy Commanders	JYB
			for training in accordance with Bn. Scheme.	JYB
	25		Coys. at disposal of Coy Comdr.	JYB
	26		Coys. at disposal of Coy Comdr. New draft of 5 signallers arrive.	JYB
			Two other signallers posted but remain at Divn signalling school.	JYB
WARLOY	27		Bn entrained at S.T RICQUIER. proceeded to ALBERT, marching thence to	JYB
			WARLOY.	JYB
	28		Coys. at disposal of Coy Comdrs. Whole Bn. goes through Gas Chamber.	JYB
MONTAUBAN	29	11.30am	Bn. journeyed by bus to MONTAUBAN arriving about 3pm.	JYB
			A new draft 27 OR. joined the Bn.	JYB
	30		Coys at disposal of Coy Comdrs.	JYB

Army Form C. 2118.

WAR DIARY
or
INTELLIGENCE SUMMARY. 1/8th Bn. The Worcestershire Regt.
(Erase heading not required.)

Copy of Original.

Place	Date	Hour	Summary of Events and Information	Remarks and references to Appendices
			The following is a list of awards made during the month of September.	
			Capt. L.R. Bomford (MC+Bar); Lt. W.E. Smedley (MC); Lt.T.L. Jones (MC)	
			Major J.P. Bate (Italian Croce de Guerra); Capt T. Sharland (Italian Bronze Medal) (MC)	
			2/Lt J.H. Greenaway (Italian Silver Medal); 2/Lt C. Brown (Italian Bronze Medal).	
			240119 Sergt Sherwood (DCM+Italian Bronze Medal); 240043 Sergt Bradley MM	
			240381 Sergt Guest C (MM); 260193 L/Sergt Worland J (MM)	
			2639 L/Cpl Price W (MM); 240896 Cpl Oleman T.K. (MM)	
			241755 Pte Sangar W.B (MM)(Bar) 39890 Pte Rock J.L (MM)	
			242441 Pte Skinner J (MM) 241594 Pte Horner J.H (MM)	
			241592 Pte Turner H (MM).	

H.J. Clarke
Lieut. Col.
Commanding 1/8th Bn. The Worcestershire Regt.

Army Form C. 2118.

WAR DIARY
INTELLIGENCE SUMMARY.
(Erase heading not required.)

Vol 43

1/8th Bn. The Worcestershire Regt.

Place	Date 1918 Oct.	Hour	Summary of Events and Information	Remarks and references to Appendices
Combles	1		The Battalion moved to Combles	Appx (A)
Norlu	2		The Battalion moved to Norlu	
S.t Emilie	3		The Battalion marched to S.t Emilie arriving 8 p.m. and billeted in a field	
	4		Marched to obstructions E. of Guennemont Farm starting at 3 p.m.	
Beaurevoir	5		The Battalion moved from Guennemont Farm to M.t S.t Martin Leur the Battalion August in the side of the road about mid-day and moved off again at 4 p.m. to attack Beaurevoir on the following formation A Coy Right B Coy Left, C Coy Rgt Support D Coy Left Support with the 5th Glos B.n on the right. The attack was launched at 6.30 p.m. the enemy put down a very barrage and numerous M.Gs were active. Beaurevoir was captured.	(Appx B) (C) (+)
"	6		Battalion held outskirts of Beaurevoir	
"	7		Battalion Lear was taken over by Regts of 66th Div: preparatory to attack by 12th moved to trenches behind Beaurevoir	
Ponchaux	8		The B.n moved to Ponchaux in close support to the 66th Division	
	9		Orders were given the Objective of the Battalion being Railway and Honnechy the advance was made in artillery formation as far as Maretz at Maretz the Battalion deployed to attack high ground in front of Honnechy the	(A)

WAR DIARY
or
INTELLIGENCE SUMMARY.   1/8th Bn. The Worcestershire Regt.

(Erase heading not required.)

Army Form C. 2118.

Place	Date	Hour	Summary of Events and Information	Remarks and references to Appendices
HONNECHY	1918 Oct. 9		The forward was repeated with enemy M.Gs. and the advance was held up for some time by careful manoeuvring and daring work by individual men the high ground was taken and HONNECHY completely captured by about 6 p.m.	Appendix (H)
"	10		The Battalion received orders to move 800x in rear of the 1/5 Glo. Regt. who were continuing the attack towards LE CATEAU. The enemy was found to be holding his outpost line very strongly and the attack was held up. The Battalion dug in on the side of a Sunken Road at Q.19.a. (Sheet 57 B SE)	H.Q.
"	11		The Battalion was relieved by the 7th WILTS (50th Div.) and marched to billets in HONNECHY.	" (I) H.Q.
SERAIN	12		The Battalion moved to Billets in SERAIN	" K H.Q.
"	13		Resting & cleaning	H.Q.
"	14		The P.C.C. addressed the troops saying how proud of them he was.	H.Q.
"	15		The Battalion was reorganised into 3 Companies 'B' Co. be absorbed into A C & D each of these Companies was organised into 3 platoons	H.Q.
HONNECHY	16		Battalion moved to HONNECHY at 3.30 p.m.	H.Q. "L"
"	17	7 a.m.	The Battalion moved to Sunken Road Q.19.a (Sheet 57 B S.E.) in support to	" M

Army Form C. 2118.

WAR DIARY
or
INTELLIGENCE SUMMARY.
(Erase heading not required.)

1/8th Bn. The Worcestershire Regt.

Place	Date	Hour	Summary of Events and Information	Remarks and references to Appendices
	1918 Octo.			
HINNECHY (Sunken Road)	17		The 50th Division in their attack on the high ground S. of LE CATEAU.	31-16
	18		Still in Sunken Road awaiting Orders	(M)eudon 1/11/16
ST BENIN	19		The Battalion moved at 2.30 am to Railway Cutting to go through 50th Division	" (N) 31-16
			and capture BASUEL. The attack was started in a thick mist. the Battalion	" (O)
			deployed and went through the 50th Div. The operation was most successful	
			all objectives being gained by 3 p.m.	31-16
BASUEL	20		The Battalion was relieved after assist. by the 5th Leinsters (6th Div.) and moved	" (P) 31-16
ST BENIN	21		back to ST BENIN	
	22		The Bn. moved to railway cutting (at 10.30 P.M.) S.E. of LE CATEAU preparing	" (Q) 31-16
			to an attack forming a flank guard for the 18th Div. on the N. end of EVEQUE	
EVEQUE Wood	23		WOOD. During this operation the town & village of POMMEREUIL was	" (R) 31-16
			captured by 'A' Coy.	
FONTAINE	24		The Battalion moved forward to establish a line on the N. of FONTAINE, which village	" (S) 31-16 1930
	25		was captured at about 7 A.M.	" (T) 31-16
POMMEREUIL	26		On the evening of the 25th the Battalion was relieved by 2 Coys of the 20th Manchesters	" (U) 31-16
			and moved back to POMMEREUIL. The Divisional General attended the B's our next Parade & complimented the Battalion on the excellent work the Battalion had done.	31-16

Army Form C. 2118.

WAR DIARY
INTELLIGENCE SUMMARY
(Erase heading not required.)

1/8th Bn. The Worcestershire Regt.

Place	Date	Hour	Summary of Events and Information	Remarks and references to Appendices
POMMEREUIL	1918 Oct 27		Resting	
"	28		" Leaving	
"	29		" Reinft of 14 O.R. joined the Battalion	
"	30		" out Ammunition training	
"	31		" two drafts arrived 2 Officers 188 O.R. and 59 O.R. Battalion was reconstituted into 4 Coys of 3 platoons. The C.O. addressed the Battalion in the afternoon.	

Attached :- Copy of message from Bn Co Commanding 7th Bn 1st Cdn Offensive
Total Casualties, Officers Drafts :- W

H J Clarke
Lieut. Col.
Commanding 1/8th Bn. The Worcestershire Regt.

1/8 Bn. The Worcestershire Regt.
Narrative of Operations, 5 October 1918

Ref. 62B 1/40,000.

1. On the morning of 5.X.18. the Bn. moved forward from near Quennement Farm (A.30.c) to just south of MT. ST MARTIN (A.18.d) and the 1/5th Glouc. Regt. to LORMISSET (B.14.a)

2. At 3 p.m. verbal orders were received from the G.O.C. Brigade to attack BEAUREVOIR in cooperation with the 1/5 Glouc. on the right. The 7th and 74th Brigades were then holding a line about 100 yds. W. of BEAUREVOIR with BELLEVUE FARM held by the 9th Yorks.

3. The Bn. moved forward at 4.30 p.m. with A Coy. on the right B. left, D right support, C left support (See OO 91 Appendix A)

4. We advanced in artillery formation up to a point just short of the top of the ridge about B.14 b.5.7 where we waited for the Barrage to open. During the time of waiting, the Company and Platoon Commanders crawled to the top of the ridge, looked at the ground and made their final plans for the attack.

5. At 6.15 p.m. the barrage opened and we advanced through the line of posts held by the 9th Yorks. The enemy immediately opened a very heavy counter-barrage and one shell hit 'D' Coy. H.Q. wounding Lt. T.L. JONES (Coy. Comdr.) and killing C.S.M. WHEELER. About 6.30 p.m. the leading wave had reached the barrage but as it was not timed to lift until 6.40 p.m. they had to lie down and wait.
The enemy held the line of the railway cutting and embankment in B.9.d. also a high bank, some pits & houses on the W. of the Village with M.G's which met the leading Coys. with very heavy fire. Several of these M.G.s were very difficult to locate and although 'A' and 'B' Coys. retaliated with L.G. fire, B. Coy. suffered very heavy casualties while waiting for the barrage to lift, Capt C.H. SMITH being wounded twice and a large number of N.C.O.s killed + wounded.

6. 2/Lieut E. WEDGBURY, o/c N°13 Platoon, D Coy, seeing that A Coy. was held up by the M.G.s in the railway cutting, took his platoon round the right flank and attacked the enemy from the rear, capturing one M.G. and 36 prisoners. 2/LT. G.H. BARBER o/c N°3 Platoon then pushed on up the village street, putting out of action a M.G. in the Square and consolidated a line to the East of the village, also gaining touch with the 1/5 Glouc. on the right.

7. LT. WATKINSON with the remainder of A Coy. followed through the village, mopping up on the way and extended the line to the left. 2/LT. WEDGBURY with 2 platoons of D Coy co-operated (See para 14)

8. In the mean time, 'C' Coy. whose role was to form defensive flank on the N. side of the village, advanced to the right of BELLEVUE FME where they were met by very heavy enfilade M.G. fire. Lts HAWTREY and GUNDRY being wounded and the leading platoons suffering very heavy casualties. Capt. WALFORD however, pushed on with third platoon, gained touch with the 9th Yorks' post at BELLEVUE FME and commenced to build up a defensive flank facing NORTH. A gap, however, still remained between his right, and the left A and D Coys. He sent out patrols to gain touch and came to Bn H.Q. to report. I then sent Lieut. WILES with the survivors of 'B' Coy., and 2/Lt. HALES with the remaining Platoon of D Coy. to mop up the North end of the village and fill in gap in the line in B.4.d. At the same time I sent Lieut. MILLER (Bn L.G. Officer) to ascertain the situation on the East side of the village: as a result of his report I sent the Adjutant (Capt GILBERT) to reorganise the line of defence with A.B & C Coys in the front line, each with a platoon of D Coy. in support. He found that LT WATKINSON had taken command of the situation in our part of the village, gained touch with the left Coy. Comndr. of 1/5 Gloucs. and established his H.Q. near the Church.

9. Later, on hearing that 2 Coys. of the 1/8 R. Warwicks, who had been attached to the 9th Yorks. were being withdrawn to LORMISSET I asked the G.O.C. Brigade to leave one Coy. with me as Bn. Resve. which he did.

10. Map of dispositions at 11 p.m. 5×18 attached (see Appendix B.)

11. Our casualties, so far as at present ascertained, were as follows:-

	Officers.	Other Ranks.	
	Wounded.	Killed	Wounded.
A Company	1.	6	17.
B "	1.	13.	32.
C "	2.	7.	32.
D "	1.	2.	22.
Bn Hd. Qrs.	-	-	5.
	5.	28.	108.

12. Captures:

	Prisoners.	Machine Guns.
A Company	100.	2.
B "	50	-
C "	3	.
D "	50	3.
Bn Hd Qrs.	2.	
	205.	

Note. About one other gun was abandoned by the enemy, but not salved by us.

13. About 7.30 p.m Lieut REDHEAD of the Manchester Regt. (7th Bde.) who had already made one attack on BEAUREVOIR that day reported to Lt WATKINSON with about 30 men and rendered valuable assistance in consolidating the line N.E. of the village.

13. X. 18.

H.T.Clarke
Lt-Colonel
Comndg. 1/8th Battalion
The Worcestershire Regt.

Secret   Copy No. 11

1/8th Bn. The Worcestershire Regt.
Operation Order No. 87

1:10:1918.

INFORMATION 1. The Brigade will move to COMBLES area to-day.
INTENTION 2. The Battalion will move to COMBLES area to-day.
INSTRUCTIONS 3.(a.) The Battalion will assemble in Column of Route, Lead of Column by 'B' Coy. Billets facing WEST at 0900
(b.) Order of March: Drums, Hd Qrs, 'B' 'A' 'C' 'D' Coy, Transport.
(c.) Dress. Marching Order. Shrapnel Helmets on back of pack.
(d.) Route. GUILLEMONT - COMBLES.
(e.) Distances. Between each Coy, 100 yds, each group of 6 vehicles, 25 yds.
(f.) Transport. Cookers to be ready by 0800
(g.) Baggage. All Baggage to be at Q.M. Stores by 07.30
(h.) Billeting Party. Lieut. R.S. MILLER and 5 Signallers will meet Staff Captain at Area Comdt's Office at 0900. ↘ COMBLES.
(j.) Reports to Head of Column.
(k.) ACKNOWLEDGE.

E. Gillut. Capt. Adjt
1/8th Bn. The Worcestershire Regt

Secret

1/8th Bn. The Worcestershire Regt.
Operation Order No. 88.

Copy No. 11
(6)

Ref: LENS, 11. 1/100,000
VALENCIENNE, 12. 1/100,000

2.10.1918.

INFORMATION 1. The Brigade will proceed to NURLU Area, to-day.

INTENTION 2. The Battalion will march to NURLU Area, to-day.

INSTRUCTIONS 3.(a) <u>Order of March</u>: Drums, 'C', 'D', Hd. Qrs 'A', 'B' Coys., Transport.
 (Coy. Lewis Gun Limber will move in rear of its Coy. and
 1 Bn. Hd. Qr. Gun will be mounted for A.A.)
 (b) <u>Dress</u>: Marching Order.
 (c) <u>Starting Point</u>: Entrance to Camp, on road.
 (d) <u>Time</u>: 1220.
 (e) <u>Route</u>: COMBLES — BOUCHAVESNES — MOISLAINS.
 (f) <u>Distances</u>: As for yesterday.
 (g) <u>Baggage</u>: Officers' valises and Mess boxes to be at Q.M. Stores
 by 1115. Blankets stacked near to the road, entrance to Camp.
 (1 Mess Box per Coy to be at Hd. Qrs by 1130.)
 (h) <u>Billeting Party</u>. 2/Lieut. J.H. GREENAWAY and 5 Signallers will meet
 Staff Captain at Area Commandant's Office NURLU at 1400.

REPORTS. 4. To Head of Column.
 (a) ACKNOWLEDGE

Distribution:
Copy No 1 - C.O.
 " 2 - 2nd in Command.   Copy No 9 - T.O.
 " 3-7 - Coys   " 10 - R.S.M.
 " 8 - S.M.   " 11 - War Diary
                           " 12 - File

R. Gilbert, Capt. & Adjt,
1/8th Bn. The Worcestershire Regt.

Secret.   1/8th Bn. The Worcestershire Regt.   Copy 191.
             Operation Order No 89.   C

Ref. ST. QUENTIN
12. 1/100,000   3.10.18
& Sheet 62c.

INFORMATION 1. The Brigade is moving to St EMILE
             Area to-day.

INTENTION   2. The Battalion will march to St EMILE
             to-day.

             (a)
INSTRUCTIONS 3. Order of March: 'D' 'A' H.Q's, Drums
             'B' 'C' Coys, Transport.
             (Coy. Lewis Guns in rear of Coy.)
             (b) Dress. Marching Order

             (c) Starting Point. D.4.a.88.
             (d) Time. 1810.
             (e) Route. LIERAMONT -
                 VILLERS FAUCON - St EMILE
             (f) Distances. As for yesterday
             (g) Baggage. Q.M. Stores by 1730
                 Mess boxes on Mess Cart

REPORTS   4. (a) To head of Column
             (b) ACKNOWLEDGE.

Distribution:
NORMAL
                                      Capt & Adjt.,
                              1/8th Bn. The Worcestershire Regt.

SECRET 1/8"?" The Worcestershire R.
Operation Order No 90.

Ref Montbrehain
1-20,000
                                            4-10-18

INTENTION. 1. The Battalion will march to S. of QUENNEMONT FARM. To-day.

INSTRUCTIONS. 2. (a) Order of March 'C' 'B' Coys. H⁰ 90, A.D. Coy Transport
(b) S.P.   Entrance to Camp
(c) Time   1305
(d) Distances   as usual
(e) Route   RONSSOY – HARGICOURT

Steel helmets will be worn.

Distribution
Normal.

                        [signature] Capt & Adjt
                        1/8 The Worcestershire Rgt

1/8 Bⁿ THE WORCESTERSHIRE Regᵗ

SECRET.   Copy No. 12

Ref.   Operation Order No. 91.

Mont Brehain 1/20.000   5·10·18

Information. 1. The enemy is reported to be holding the eastern outskirts of BEAUREVOIR and the Railway cutting in B.9.d. The 9ᵗʰ Yorks Regᵗ are holding BELLEVUE FARM and a line to road 400ˣ W. BEAUREVOIR MILL. The 8ᵗʰ R. Warwickˢ Regᵗ is attacking GUISANCOURT FARM this afternoon.

Intention 2. The Battalion will attack the Northern half of BEAUREVOIR and the 5ᵗʰ Glos Regᵗ the Southern half.

Instructions 3. (a) 'A' Right Coy 'B' Coy Left 'D' Right Support 'C' Left Support. Company boundaries and objectives will be as pointed out to Company commanders on the ridge.

(b) The Battalion will form up for the attack on the line shown to Coy. Commanders on the ground at 4.30 P.M. and will

(2)

and will cross the front line of
the 9th Yorks at 6.30 P.M.
(c) Artillery barrage will commence
on the railway cutting at 6.15 P.M
and will remain stationary till
6.40 a.m. when it will advance
at the rate of 100ˣ in 6 minutes
till it forms a protective screen
in a semicircle 500ˣ to 600ˣ
outside the village.
Within the limits of the barrage
'A' Coy will establish posts
forward.

Distribution
Normal

SECRET.   Copy 12
 1/8th Bn The Worcestershire Regt.
   Operation Order 92 9.10.18.
Ref: 57B S.E. ⎫ 1/20.000
     57B S.W. ⎭
     MONTBREHAIN

INFORMATION 1 (a) The 25th Division is
continuing the attack this morning
with American troops on the right
& the 66th Division on left.
     The Div: front is now along
the road from SERAIN to PREMONT
with the left boundary on LE CATEAU
Road and PREMONT being exclusive
to Division.
     (b) The 75th Inf Bde will
attack with the 74th Bde on the Right
the first objective V.8.a 50 to V.1.b.46
being allotted to the 1/8 R.WARWICKS
and 1/5 GLOUCESTER Regt.
INTENTION (2) The Battn will cross
the above line at 8 am & capture
the line P.30.c.16 to P.23 Central

INSTRUCTIONS 3 (a). Order of march.
A, B, C Coys. A.Q's. D Coy.
Starting point B.18.a.12.
Time 3 am.
(b) The Battalion will deploy into
Artillery formation of Companies
in Column of fours on the road
U.22.c.3.4. - U.21.d.6.9. at 3.45 am
as follows:- A Right Coy. B Left
Coy. C Right Support. D Left
Support.
(c) The Battalion will advance
at the rate of 100 yards in 3
minutes moving by the left on
a frontage of 300 yards with the
Left flank on LE CATEAU Road
Thence round the Southern side
of MARETZ to the line V.1.a.68 –
V.1.b.36 when it will deploy into
Artillery formation of platoon
on a frontage of 400 yards.
(d) The first objective of the
Battalion THE RAILWAY LINE
P.34.c.28 to P.28.c.18 will be
taken by A & B Coys. C & D Coys

will then pass through & take the second objective P.30.c.16 – P.23 Central. D Coy will detail 1 Platoon to keep liaison with the 66th Division in the centre of HONNECHY. A Coy will then establish a defensive flank on the railway line about P.28.d and 29.c. B Coy will hold FIRST Objective.
(c) TANKS will probably cooperate.
REPORTS 4. Batt^n H.Q. will move in centre of last wave up to house on Light Railway at V.1.c.63 thence to QUARRY at P.33.c.89.
AID POST. 5. House at V.1.c.15.
TRANSPORT. 6. Will move with Bn to point of first deployment thence to SW end of MARETZ where it will await orders. One pack animal will move with each Coy & 2 with Bn H.Q. as far as QUARRY at P.33.c.89 where they will remain until required.

Distribution normal   Bellett Capt & Adjt
Issued by Runner 7 pm. 11.10.18 2/6 West Kent

1/8th Bn. The Worcestershire Regt.
Narrative of Operations, 9 October 1918.

Ref. 57 B & 62 B
1/40,000.

(h)

1. At 11.50 p.m. 8.X.18 at PONCHAUX, orders were received to move forward in rear of the 1/5 Glouc. Regt. who were attacking MARETZ and at 8 a.m. on 9.X.18. to move forward from the latter place and capture HONNECHY with the 74th Bde. forming a defensive flank on the right and the 66 Divn. attacking MAUROIS on the left.

2. At 5 a.m. the Bn formed up on the SERAIN–PREMONT road (then held by the 4th Bde) with our left flank on the LE CATEAU Road. Order of Coys:— A right, B left, C right support, D left support. (See OO 92 Appendix A.)

3. At 5.20 a.m. the 1/5 Glouc. moved forward behind the creeping barrage and at 8.45 a.m. we followed behind them in artillery formation. It soon became evident that our barrage was falling short, most of it being behind the 1/5 Glouc. and the shells from one 4.5 How. and one 18 pdr. gun bursting very short as a result of which the right platoon of A Coy. suffered 4 casualties and 2/Lt. BROWN who was walking by my side in the centre of the leading wave, was wounded.

4. The 1/5 Glouc. captured MARETZ without opposition, but although we passed through them as soon as the barrage allowed, we did no reach our next jumping off line in V.1.b. until 8.30 a.m. We then continued the advance but had not gone far before heavy M.G. fire was opened from the railway about V.3.c.7.1. and from the woods and houses in P.26 and 27. One platoon of C Coy under Lt. WATSON attacked and drove off the M.G.s on the railway but the others continued to give trouble and were holding up the 66th Divn. troops on the N. side of the LE CATEAU road. However, by skilful use of cover afforded by undulating ground the advance was continued up to the Quarry and road in P.33 a. and c.

5. Large numbers of our cavalry then deployed from behind MARETZ and moved forward and the enemy commenced to shell the whole area rather heavily.

6. As the attack appeared to be held up I went forward to the Quarry in P.33c. where I ascertained that the 74th Bde were holding the railway line in V.3. and the 66th Divn had with the assistance of 2 Armoured Cars advanced to the Eastern edge of the wood in P.27 but that further progress on our front was rendered difficult by M.G. fire from the railway in P.28 c. and P.34 a.

7. The 21st Manchesters (7th Inf. Bde) had also come forward during the morning and after consultation with their C.O. and my Coy. Comdrs. I decided that a concerted attack with a barrage would be the best method of dealing with the situation. I therefore arranged for a barrage on the railway from 1.55 to 2.0 p.m. and an assault at 2 p.m. the 21st Manchesters to fill in the gap on our right; I also wrote to the O.C. Right Bn. 66th Divn. asking him to co-operate.

8. While these arrangements were being made, the enemy withdrew his M.G.s, but it took some time to countermand the barrage and the advance of our troops was therefore delayed and the enemy got away.

9. At 2 p.m. A and B Coys. occupied their objective, (the railway line) and C and D Coys. passed through to the village.
The cavalry also moved forward at the same time and several enemy batteries to the E. and S.E. of the village shelled them at very short range causing some casualties to our men.

10. C and D Coys. consolidated on the line of the road in P.23 d., 29 b. and 30 a. and A Coy. formed a defensive flank about the station in P.29 d. B Coy. remained in Bn. Reserve in the railway cutting in P.28.C.
(See map attached. Appendix B)

11. Our casualties.

	Officers	Other Ranks	
	Wounded	Killed	Wounded
A Company	-	1	20
B "	1	1	21
C "	1	3	19
D "	1	-	15
Bn. Hd Qrs.	-	-	3
	3	5	68

12. Captures.
A large amount of rolling stock and other materiel at HONNECHY railway station.

12: X: 18.

H. T. Clarke.
Lt. Colonel
Commandg. 1/8th Battalion
The Worcestershire Regt.

To O.C. A Worcestershire Regt.
Operation Order No. 98.

SECRET Copy No. 11
Map Sheet 57° SE SW. 10.10.18

INFORMATION 1. The Bn. is being relieved to-day
the Battalion on the relief by 3 Coys
of the 7th Wilts

INTENTION 2.(a) On relief Coys will move to
HONNECHY

INFORMATION 3.(a) Coys will move off as ordered
C. Coy will move on arrival of
C. Coy of 7. Wilts and will not be chum
(b) Guides will meet Coys at the
Square on arrival
(c) Lewis Guns will be loaded
on Limbers outside C. Coy at 5.30 pm
(d) Relief complete will be sent
to Bn. go before moving off.

[signed]
18th Battn.

1/8 Bn. The Worcestershire Regt.
Operation Order No 94

Ref. Sheet 57B. S.W.   11-10-18

Infmtn. 1. The Bde. is moving to SERAIN to-day.

Intentn. 2. The Bn. moves to SERAIN to-day.

Instrtns 3. (a) Order of March H.Q., A. B. C. D. Transpt.
(b) Time 1430.
(c) Starting Pt. Bn. Hd. Qrs.
(d) Dress. Marchg. Order.
(e) Distances 100ˣ between Companies.
(f) Billetg. Party. 5 Signallers under MAJOR BATE meet Staff Capt. at SERAIN Church at 1300.
(g) Guides will meet Coys. on arrival
(h) Transpt. B Echelon moves in rear of Column joining Col. at MARETZ

Reports 4. To head of Column.

Dist: (Sd.) E. GILBERT. Capt & Adjt
NORMAL   1/8 Bn The Worcestershire Regt

1/8 Bn. The Worcestershire Regt.
Operation Order No 95

Secret.

Copy No 11

16.10.18

Map Ref. Sheet 57b 1/40,000

Information 1.		The Bn will move to HONNECHY To-day.
Intention 2.		The Battalion will march to HONNECHY To-day.
Instructions 3.	Order of March:	'A' Coy H.Qrs. Drums 'C' 'D' Coys. Section of T.M.Bs TRANSPORT. 'B' Echelon.
		(Lewis Gun limber in rear of each Company)
	Starting Point:	Orderly Room.
	Time.	13.25
	Distances :	100 yards between Coys. and between sections of 6 vehicles
	Dress :	Fighting Order (Packs instead of haversacks)
	Billeting Party	2Lt BATEMAN and 4 Runners (with cycles) report to Staff Capt. HONNECHY CHURCH 15.30.
		Blankets, Officers Kit (Surplus) Greatcoats, and mess boxes less ONE for company. to be dumped at Billet No 12 by 14.00 Valises and Mess Boxes at Stores by 14.15
Reports 4.		To head of Column.
		Acknowledge

Distribution
Copy. No 1. C.O
2. 2 i/C
3-6 Coys
7 T.O.
8 Q.M.
9 A S.M
10 File
11 War D.

E. Gilbert. Capt. and Adjt

1/8 Bn The Worcestershire Regt.

SECRET.

1/8 Bn. The Worcestershire Regt.
OPERATION ORDER No. 96

Copy No. M
17.10.18

INFORMATION 1. The 75th Bde is in Reserve to the XIII Corps.
The Battalion will be in reserve to the 150th Bde.

INTENTION 2. The Battalion will move forward to SUNKEN ROAD in Q.19a

INSTRUCTIONS 3. Order of March.   HQ 97 "C" "D" "A" Coys Sec T.M.Bs. Pack Animals
Starting Point.   Road junction P.23.C.3½
Time   0820
Distances.   As for yesterday
Dress   Fighting Order. Lewis Guns will be carried
Transport.   Transport will be parked at present billet
                  and will await further orders.

Reports: 4. To Q.19.C.99.

                                        [signature]
                                        Capt. & Adjt.
                                        1/8th Bn. The Worcestershire Regt.

Secret   Copy No. 8.

1/8th Bn. The Worcestershire Regt.
Operation Order No 97.

Ref. Map. 57B.
1/40,000.   18.10.18.

INFORMATION 1. The attack will be renewed at ZERO hour this morning when the 50th Divn. will advance from the Red Dotted Line reaching the Red Line at ZERO plus 63 mins. The 75th B'de. will capture the Blue Line.

INTENTION 2. The Bn. with the 5th Gloucs. on the left will capture the line of the Road from R.9.c.1.3. to R.7.b.7.9. inclusive.

INSTRUCTIONS 3.(a) The Bn. will assemble as follows:—

(b) Route. Road through Q.19.d. to Q.26.a., Q.26.d. central Q.27.c.,a. & b. over Bridge in Q.28.c.

(c) Starting Point. X Roads Q.19.d.0.9.

(d.) Time: 0245.

(e) Assembly Position. Pt about Q.29.a.00., 400ˢ due East of R'way to the bridge Q.22.b.21. 'C' Right Coy. 'D' Centre, 'A' Left Coy., D Coy 1/8 R. Warwicks Regt. will be in Battn. Reserve.

(f) Objectives. 'C' Coy. Bend in road at R.9.c.1.3. to X Roads R.8.b.7.4.
D Coy. To Bridge over stream at R.8.a.7.6.
'A' Coy to HALTE at R.7.b.7.9. (inclusive)
D Coy., 1/8 R. Warwicks if not otherwise involved will consolidate on the semi-circular Road from R.8.c.3.0. to R.7.d.7.8.

LIAISON 4. Flank Coys. will detail 1 section each, to maintain liaison, in accordance with instructions.

AID POSTS 5.(a.) Q.22.b.4.1.

(b) Road junction Q.1.3.d.8.4.

TRANSPORT 6. Will receive orders through B'de. Hd. Qrs.

REPORTS 7. (a) Q.22.b.21.

(b) Q.17.c.9.4.

(c) Q.12.d.9.4.

Distribution:—
C.O.   No. 1.
Coys.   - 2-4.
T.O.   - 5.
R.S.M.   - 6.
File   - 7.
W. Diary   - 8.

                                    Capt. & Adjt.,
                          1/8th Bn. The Worcestershire Regt.

1/8 Bn. The Worcestershire Regt.
Narrative of Operations 18 Oct. 1918
Ref Sheet 57 ᴮ S.E. 1/20,000.

1. At 3 a.m. on 18 x 18 the Battalion moved forward from the road in Q 19 a to the railway cutting in Q 22 c where it formed up with the 1/5 Glos. Regt on the left, and the 1/8 Bn. R. Warwickshire Regt (less one company) in Bn. Reserve. D Coy 1/8 R. Warwick Regt was attached to the Battalion (B Coy had been temporarily disbanded to make the other companies up to fighting strength.)

2. Order of Coys. 'C' on right 'D' Centre 'A' Left. 'D' Coy R. Warwicks in Bn. Res.

3. The 149th and 151st Bde. 50th Division were holding the line of the road in Q 17 a & 23 b & d. The 150th Bde. were forming up on this line to attack a line along the ridge in Q 12 b R 7 c 13 a & c 19 a, with the Americans conforming on their right.

4. The 75th Bde. were ordered to follow up the 150th Bde. go through them and capture BASUEL and the line of Railway Cutting running west from the village.

5. 5.30 a.m. was zero hour for the 150th Bde. and as soon as our barrage opened the enemy replied on the area in Q 22 a & c with a heavy H.E. and gas bombardment (one H.E. shell inflicted 18 casualties on No. 4 Platoon A Coy)

6. At 7.15 a.m. the Battalion moved forward in Artillery formation but owing to the dense fog A Coy quickly lost touch with D Coy and failed at first to gain touch with the Gloucesters. They pushed on, however, to the road in Q 18 a & d and as the fog then lifted they gained touch with the Gloucesters and continued the advance.
They were fired on by M.Gs. on the right flank but pressed on leaving them to be dealt with by the other companies.

(2)   18 x 18

7. On reaching the high ground in R.7.c. 'A' Coy was met by heavy enfilade M.G. fire and direct fire from 77 m.m. gun at 400 yards range. Lieut Reynolds opened fire with his Lewis Guns and drove the enemy gunners away.

8. At this point the Company Commander of 'D' Coy R. Warwicks (Lieut FAWKE) came up and gained touch with 'A' Coy (Lieut WATKINSON) who asked him for two platoons to protect the right flank. D & C Coys being still held up in Q.18 b & d and R.13 a & c.

9. 'A' Coy then pushed on to the village joining up with the Gloucesters, who were on their objective the railway embankment in Q.6.d and R.1 c & d, but 'A' Coy were not in sufficient force to progress far, and had to wait for the other two companies to advance.

10. On receiving a message that C & D Companies were held up (as stated in para 8) by M.G. fire from the front and the right flank and that the troops on their right were also unable to advance I asked the G.O.C. 13th for another Company of the Warwicks which he gave me. I ordered them to go round the left of 'D' Coy and attack the enemy M.Gs from the North. In the meantime, however, Capt WALFORD O.C. 'C' Coy. had made a personal reconnaissance and decided to advance firing Lewis Guns and Rifle from the hip. This smothered the enemy fire and the attack was successfully continued right through the village to the objective. On the way 'C' Coy captured a complete Battery of 4.2" Howitzers with the battery commander and 18 horses. Later they also captured two ammunition limbers and 6 horses which were coming into the village from CATILLON.

(3)   18.X.18

11. When O.C. A Coy saw C & D advancing, he also advanced and reached his objective. Several M.Gs. were encountered in the village and on the railway embankment and were either captured or driven out by L.G. and rifle grenade fire.

12. By 3 p.m. all Force Companies had gained their objectives, "mopped up" the village and started to consolidate.
   (See sketch map attached)

13. Our Casualties

	Officers Wounded	Other Ranks Killed	Other Ranks Wounded
	1	2	38

14. Captures

	Prisoners	Horses	Guns	M.Gs.
A Coy	7		1	5
C Coy	107 + 28	24	4	
D Coy	49		3	
	107 + 78	24	8	5

Also C Coy   4 Gun Limbers & 40 Railway trucks
     D Coy   1 Baggage Wagon

H. T. Clarke
Lt. Col.
Commanding 1/8th Worcestershire Regt.

23.10.18.

Disposition 1/4th Worcester Regt
Oct 18 to 19

To ORS

Triple N Cateau

A Coy   D Coy

D Coy
Rifle Works   BASUEL   To ORS

To CATILLON

From ST BENIN

Bⁿ HQrs at
G 18 d 3 6

To BAZINEHIEN

H H Clarke

1/8 Bn. The Worcestershire Rgt. (P)
Operation Order No 98.
Secret.   20.10.18
Ref Sheet 57ᵇ S.E.

INFORMATION 1. The Battalion will be relieved
by the 1st Bn. Leicester Regt.

INTENTION 2. On relief the Bn. will march back
to Billets at ST BENIN.

INSTRUCTIONS 3. (a) GUIDES will meet Companies
at the Broken Railway Bridge
ST BENIN.
(b) TRANSPORT. Lewis Gun Limbers
will be at X Roads Q.18.a.9.4.
2 Mules will report to Bn H.Qrs
at R.7.a.3.8. at 17.30

REPORTS Relief Complete to be reported
to Bn. H.Qrs on moving off,
by Runners.

Gilbert Cartwright
1/8 Bn. The Worcestershire Rgt.

Amendment to O.O. 99. of 22.10.18

1. Cancel sub paras (a) and (b) of para 3 and substitute:-
Battalion will parade in Column of Route facing East. Head of Column on Road junction just outside Q.M. Stores at 22.00. Order. Bn H.Q. C D A. Lewis Guns will be carried from here.

2. Battn will move to Railway Cutting in Q.6.d. arriving before 00.30.

3. On arrival in cutting Coy Comdrs will report to Bn H.Q. on the Right of Battn. Order of Coys in cutting Right to Left C D A

Battalion will move forward from Cutting following route originally laid down on orders from Commanding Officer.

2/10/18.

Kellet
Capt & Adjt
1/8th Bn The Worc Regt.

Addendum to O.O. 99 of 22.10.18.

1.
1 Section of 4 TANKS will follow the Battalion assisting to establish posts and to capture the FARM LESTILLEUX. Each TANK will carry 5 boxes S.A.A available for Infantry.

2.
There will be a cessation of fire for 5 minutes prior to the time fixed for the commencement of the barrages in front of the first and succeeding objectives, and 4 minutes intense fire before the barrage lifts, in order to indicate the hour of next advance.

22/10/18

Gilbert Capt & Adjt
1/8th Bn. The Worc. Regt.

SECRET   AM(Q)/15
         Copy No........

/8th Bn The Worcestershire Regt
Operation Order No 99.   22.10.18.

Ref: 57.B. NE. } 1/20,000
     57.B. SE. }

1. **INFORMATION.** (a) 18th Division on our Left (53rd Bde on Right of 18th Div) are attacking North of BOIS L'EVEQUE; boundary as shown on map
   (b) 1/5 GLOUCESTERS on our Right are attacking and holding line from L.21.a.00 to L.16.b.69. after first objective has been made good by 75th Brigade.
   (c) Attack will move at rate of 100 yards to 6 min. through wood, pausing for 40 min. on dotted blue line (FLAQUET BRIFAUT). It will move at rate of 100 yards to 4 min. on 18th Division front, pausing for 112 min. on dotted blue line (LES TILLEULS).

2. **INTENTION.** The Battalion will protect the flank of 53rd Brigade advancing with them, leaving posts to guard exits from wood at following points:
   1. Bulge in edge of wood L.20.b.70.
   2. Copse L.21.a.
   3. Spur L.15.c.73.
   4. TILLEUL FARM.
   5. Spur L.16.b.77 in touch with 53rd Brigade and with 1/5 GLOSTER Regt.

3. **DETAIL** (a) Assembly. Battalion will assemble on line of road through Q.18.central, right of Battn on hedge Q.18.a.46. in artillery formation of platoons on front of 130 yards. Companies in depth of 100 yards in order: Bn HQ. C. D. 'A' Coys
   (b) At Z-60min Battn will move forward. (Bn HQ will direct up to ORCHARD in L.26.a.) Route West of BASUEL - W and N.W. of POMMEREUIL - Edge of wood in L.20.d.
   (c) At Z+160 Battalion will reform on a one Company front of 400 yards in order C. D. A. Left of Battn on Cross roads L.20.d.19. Right: 100 yards inside edge of B. L'EVEQUE.
   (d) At Z+180 C Coy will move forward under barrage with 53rd Brigade, attack and hold points 1. 2. and 3.
   (e) 'D' Coy will move forward under barrage and attack and hold point 4. sending back guides as soon as this is done, to Battn HQ for 4 Vickers to assist in holding this point. At Z+370 2 platoons of 'D' Coy advance, capture and hold point 5, gaining touch with troops on left and right. 1 Trench Mortar will move with 'D' Coy, carrying 16 rounds.
   (f) 'A' Coy will remain in Reserve in L.20.d. O/C 'A' Coy will report to Battn HQrs as soon as in position.

4. **PACK ANIMALS.** Pack animals will move in rear of 'A' Coy.
   1 carrying Signals
   3   "   S.A.A.
   2   "   T.M. Ammunition.

5. **AID POST.** Aid Post in vicinity of Battn H.Qrs

6. **TRANSPORT.** Details will be issued later.

7. **REPORTS.** Reports to Battn H.Q. about L.20.d.45

                                        [signature]
                                        Capt & Adjt
                                        /8th Bn The Worcestershire Regt

Distribution.
No.1. Comdg Officer   No.11. 1/8 R. War.
2-4 Coys   12. 53rd Bde.
5.   L.G.O.   13. 8. R. Berks.
6-7. T.O. & art.   14. A' Coy M.G.Bn
8.   M.O.   15. Filed
9.   75th Bde.   16. War Diary.
10. 1/5 Glos.

Oct. 23.   **1918**

Narrative of operations resulting in capture of POMMEREUIL and formation of a defensive flank along N.W. edge of BOIS L'EVEQUE.

Off (R)

1. At 2200 the Battalion left ST BENIN and marched to railway cutting in Q.6.d.

2. At 0155 the leading Coy, "C" Coy preceded by LIEUT MILLER and eight men to act as guides, left the cutting at Q.6.d.6.5. followed by D and A Coy (Reserve Coy).

3. C & D Coys moved forward, ignoring various enemy posts in L.31, as these were to be dealt with by other troops. In L.25.d these companies came under heavy machine gun fire from edge of orchard in L.25.d. This position was rushed and enemy retired leaving 4 M.G.s behind. The advance was continued and enemy were met with in practice trenches in L.26.a. These latter retired leaving one M.G. behind. At 0355 the jumping off position was reached (cross roads L.20 central) and our men remained waiting for barrage to lift.

4. LIEUT MILLER and four of his eight guides (see para 2) led them at - 20 yards in front of Lodge R.6.07, so the two companies arrived at the jumping off place without guides.

5. Action of A Coy (Reserve Coy) who had been ordered to move to a position of readiness in L.20.d.
   Left cutting in Q.6.d at 0145. They came under considerable M.G. fire from L.31 & 26. Company halted at R.1.6.36 and as enemy posts were all round them sent forward scouts to find gaps in enemy line of posts. This was done and RICHEMONT stream was crossed at J. JACQUES in front while an enemy post of ten men was captured. —

6. "A" Coy then pushed on to road at L.25 d 80, coming under fire from L.32 a. and d. They then turned East and proceeded to POMMEREUIL and came under fire from L.26 c 54. A halt was again made, and a patrol was sent forward to find in what direction progress could be made. An enemy post of two men was found in house at L.26 c 01. They were killed. —

7. At 0400 the mist lifted, and "A" Coy pushed on in direction of L.20 d passing an enemy post of two M.G. firing from L.26 c 54 towards 18 Div. area. This post later surrendered to a prisoners escort coming back with a batch of prisoners. The company then established its H.Q. at L.20 d.

8. Officer commanding this Coy then came to the conclusion that POMMEREUIL was still in the hands of the enemy, and that the enemy did not know that "A" Coy were there.
   Two enemy officers, one of high rank, and their orderlies met O.C. "A" Coy on the road. These two officers put up a good fight, but were killed, one of the orderlies escaped; soon after his escape a mob of about 30 Germans ran back from the village.
   They were fired on. — Accordingly a patrol was sent into the village, and returned reporting many of the enemy there. We did not think it was advisable to enter the village, lest the enemy should see how few men were there. —

9. At about 0600 liaison was made with a female tank, and it was arranged to clear the village in conjunction with it. This was completed at 0700, the enemy offering little resistance. —

10. At 04.20 the barrage lifted from the starting point (cross roads L.20 central) and "C" and "D" Coy moved forward on to their objectives.

11. "C" Coy was able to take up their allotted position at L.21 a 3.6 etc. without further opposition.

12. After moving forward, about 300 yards from Pott's position, D Coy saw two guns (4.2) firing from Cot-in-d Ledge about L.16 a 3.3. These were silenced by Lewis gun and rifle fire. M.G. and rifle fire was then opened on our men, who advanced and captured their main objective, TILLEUL'S FARM, and the three 4.2 guns, killing and capturing all the team, at 0557.

13. At this time there were no troops on our right or left and the enemy S.O.S. was being sent up from 1½ miles in our rear. At dawn exceptionally pages of the St. the enemy were seen retiring on the Pott, and fire was opened. This company captured at 7.100 prisoners and several officers.

14. At 0745 East SURREYS came up on the Pott. ~~officers wounded~~ At 0800 four tanks passed through, but soon came back.

15. At 10.30 the high ground at L.16 b 6.8 which we had been holding with one section, was consolidated by two platoons.

Captures.   1 horse.
              3   4.2 long howitzers
              1   signal waggon containing signalling
                                              equipment.
              15 officers] Receipts in possession, actual
              371 O.R.   ] number must have exceeded this

Our casualties. 1 officer killed.
                 2   "   wounded
                 3 O.R.   killed
                 41 O.R.   wounded

J. S. Pigot Major

1/8" Bn Worcestershire Regt. Appx (S)
24.10.18

Narrative of operations resulting in capture of
LE GRAND qCHENEq and establishing a defensive
flank to division on Post-running from A26c91
to G2d22.

1. At 2200 at PAQUET BRIFAUT L15d54
orders were received that the Battalion was to undertake
the above operation, being attached to 74th Inf Bde for
this purpose.

2. At 0400, 24 x 18, the Battalion was formed up
400 x N.E. of TILLEULS FARM. At 0430 the advance
was commenced. At L11.c.95. the Sherwood Foresters were
found to be held up. Capt HALFORD realising
that any delay would lose the barrage carried
them forward with his men.

3. The road running through C.1.c and C.7a
was reached at 0650. 20 minutes after our barrage
had lifted. At 0655 the advance was continued
but the left Company was held up on the left
flank by M.Gs, as the left Division had
not come up. The right flank of this company
pushed on firing at the enemy who were
retiring at the double. A post was established
4. at G 26 c 9.1. according to plan.
   Enemy was seen in very large numbers,
   estimated at 400 to 500 retiring from here
   20 or 30 were killed but we had not enough
   men to surround the remainder.

4. Right Company advanced along track through
   L12a and G7a. and established posts
   at G2c98. in touch with left Company.
   An enemy M.G. at G2a 2.5. was driven back
   by L.G. fire. The Village was captured at
   least half an hour after our barrage had ceased

(2)

and this would account for so few prisoners being taken. Nearly all the enemy had time to escape to their next line of resistance on the high ground running from G.26.a to G.2.b.

5. At Midday Orders were received from 74 Inf Bde to the effect that a further advance was to be made at 1300 under a barrage to a line about 400x in front of the right Coy front. So that our front line would then run L.26.c.9.1. to G.2.d.2.1. This objective was gained at 1345 and consolidated. (6) A further

6. message received at 1300 from the 74th Inf Bde stated that ZERO would now be 1400. It was however received by companies too late for them to withdraw their men from the frontier already taken, and 5 Casualties were received from our own barrage.
Touch was then gained with the SHERWOODS on our right.

7. On the left at G.26.c.9.1. Control of the situation was kept by us up to 1100 and had the troops on our left come up a still further advance would have been easy. But the enemy finding the troops were not coming up rallied at about 1100 and harassed our men continually with M.G. fire from E. N.W. & S.W.

8. As a precaution therefore our line was withdrawn on our left flank to a wall running from G.2.c.9.8. to G.2.a.3.1.

(3)

9. At 2000 the QUEENS came up and touch was gained on the left.

<u>Our Casualties</u>

1. Officer Wounded at duty

O.R.
9. Killed
43 Wounded
1. " at duty
2 Missing

Captures. 25 Cycles
1. G.S. Wagon
3. M.Gs.
3. Prisoners.

J.P.S... Major Commanding
1/1st the Dorsetshire Regt.

Secret.   1/8 Bn. The Worcestershire Regt.   Appendix T
            Operation Order No 100.   Copy.
                                      24.10.18.

Information 1. At a time to be notified later probably early afternoon 74th Inf. Bde. will capture & consolidate a 3rd Objective which will run L.24.a.0. to track junction G.13.D.7.0. thence to X Roads G.14.c.4.4. thence to road junction G.8.d.8.5. to C.2 central (See attached map.)

Detail 2.(a) D Coy will sieze sector marked Brown acting in conjunction with 'A' Coy.

(b) Northern Boundary:- Road junction A.26.c.9.0. where mixed posts will be formed with 53 I/f Bde (7th Queens Regt.)

Southern Boundary:- from Road junction G.7.a.6.5. to G.2.d.2.3. Road & houses at G.8.a.1.7. inclusive

(c.) 11th Sherwood Foresters, 18th D.L.I., 9th Yorks will sieze sectors marked blue, red and green respectively.

(d.) Artillery programme and ZERO time will be issued later.

24.10.18   (Sd.) E. GILBERT. Capt & Adjt.,
1010   1/8 Bn. The Worcestershire Regt.

1/8 Bn The Worcestershire

SECRET.   Operation Order. No. 10
Ref Sheet 57 NE
                                        24.10.18

INFORMATION. 1. The Battalion will be relieved
                 by 2 Coys of the 20th Manchesters.

INTENTION. 2.   On relief Companies will
                 march back to billets at Pommereuil

INSTRUCTIONS. 3. Guides will meet X Roads in
                 L 20 central. To guide Coys
                 to billets
                 Guides for incoming unit
                 will be at GARAGE CORNER

Reports   4.   Relief complete to be sent
                 to 10th Hd Qrs by runner
                 when moving off.

                           [signature]
                 1/8th Bn Worcestershire
                           Rgt.

Copy.   APP (V)

75 Infantry Brigade.

From the time that the 1/8th WORCESTERSHIRE Regt came under my orders of the 24th October to support the attack of the 74th Infantry Brigade on the FINAL OBJECTIVE, the Battalion under the command of Major J.P.BATE M.C. did everything that was asked of them.

The advance was carried out in close and difficult country against stubborn resistance, the Battalion shewing great courage and determination throughout.

During this operation Major J.P.BATE M.C. showed the utmost coolness and skill in handling his Battalion and sent in excellent reports.

I wish to take this opportunity of thanking Major J.P.BATE M.C. and all ranks of the 1/8th Bn. the WORCESTERSHIRE Regt for the great assistance they rendered the Brigade in carrying out the Operation.

(Sd) H.M. CRAIGIE HALKETT Brig General
Commanding 74th Inf. Bde.

Oct: 26th 1918.

2.

O.C. 1/8 Bn. the WORCESTERSHIRE Regt.

The Brigadier General Commanding is highly gratified with this report and wishes you to communicate it to all ranks at the first opportunity

Sd. J Trencher Captain.
Staff Capt 75th Infantry Brigade

27/10/18.

APP. W.

1/8 Bn THE WORCESTERSHIRE Regt.

October. 1918

Total Casualties for the month of October. 1918

	Killed	Wounded	Missing
Officers.	3	12	
O.R.	51	313	4

Total Captures

Prisoners		M.Gs.	Guns.	Horses	Material etc.
16 Officers	657. O.R.	13	11 (Including two batteries of 4.2" Hows)	25	40 R'way Trucks. 4 Limbers 2. Baggage Wagon 1. Signal Wagon complete with equipment 25 Cycles

Also — A large quantity of Railway Rolling Stock was captured at HONNECHY.

Large Store of Bombs, Ammunition, and war material was captured during the operations.

Total of Drafts received.

8 Officers   436 O.R.

H. T. Clarke.

WAR DIARY
1/8th Bn. The Worcestershire Regt.
INTELLIGENCE SUMMARY

Army Form C. 2118.

Place	Date	Hour	Summary of Events and Information	Remarks and references to Appendices
POMMEREUIL	1918 NOVEMBER 1		Companies at disposal of Company Commanders for training	
"	2		Battalion marched to ST. BENIN to witness a demonstration of crossing a river. Afterwards a river crossing was given by D Coy. Corps & Divisional Commanders were present.	
"	3		Moved forward to Assembly Positions at MALGARNI to attack on LANDRECIES. Appx. #734	
LANDRECIES	4		At 0615 the Battalion advanced to the attack on LANDRECIES. the 1/5 GLOUC. R. and the 1/8 RL. WAR. R. Rifles were as follows. The Appendices Gloucesters and Warwicks were to make good the crossing of the SAMBRE CANAL and the 1/8 WORC. R. were to go through them, cross the CANAL capture LANDRECIES and occupy the RED Line. And push out outposts to the DOTTED RED Line. D Coy on the right advanced rapidly, crossed the CANAL on enemy bridge, captured a battery in action and were established on their line by 1115. B Coy (Left) A Coy (centre) were covering the resistance of a m.g. nest with the aid of a Tank, crossed the Canal at the lock near RR light bridge at 1245; and reached their objective shortly afterwards. C Coy (Left) advanced to the coast, overcoming heavy m.g. fire by enemy machine guns.	J.7.13 J.6.13 24.v.55

Army Form C. 2118.

(2)

WAR DIARY
or
INTELLIGENCE SUMMARY

1/8th Bn. The Worcestershire Regt.

(Erase heading not required.)

Instructions regarding War Diaries and Intelligence Summaries are contained in F. S. Regs., Part II. and the Staff Manual respectively. Title pages will be prepared in manuscript.

Place	Date	Hour	Summary of Events and Information	Remarks and references to Appendices
LANDRECIES	1918 Nov. 4		crossed the Canal on rafts under the heavy fire of guns of all sizes and every description. Hostile units 96th Pdr. 11th Bavar. Div. (right) and 149th Pdr, 3rd R.D. (left).	JR3
MAROILLES	5		In the early morning the 74th Bde continued the advance to the GREEN LINE. The Battalion with the rest of the Bde, formed a defensive flank facing S.E. as the 32nd Div. had not come up. Later in the day the Bn. moved into billets S. of MAROILLES. Reinforcements 5 O.R.	Appx. 6 & 7 JR3 JR3
"	6		Stayed at MAROILLES.	
MARBAIX	7		The 7th and 74th Bdes advanced to just E of MARBAIX and the 75th Bde went through them towards AVESNES. The battalion formed part of this main body and did not deploy. The Bn. was relieved at night by the 66th Division and moved back into billets at MARBAIX.	Appx. 8 JR3 JR3
PREUX	8		The Battalion marched to billets at PREUX, enroute passing through LANDRECIES where they were given a magnificent reception by the inhabitants who had discovered that the 1/8 WORCESTERS had captured the town. Flags & flowers were given to the men and bouquets to the (etc.)	Appx. 9 JR3

(A9479) Wt W3358/P360 600,000 12/17 D.D. & L. Sch. 52a. Forms/C2118/15.

WAR DIARY
or
INTELLIGENCE SUMMARY

(Erase heading not required.)

Army Form C. 2118.

1/8th Bn. The Worcestershire Regt.

(3)

Place	Date	Hour	Summary of Events and Information	Remarks and references to Appendices
PREUX	8		the Divisional Commander (who led the Battalion) and to the Co.	J.P.13.
"	9		Inspections and refitting	J.P.13.
"	10		Reinforcement 51 O.R.	J.P.13.
"	11		Training of specialists and company training	J.P.13.
"	12		Training as above	J.P.13.
"	13		Training as above.	J.P.13.
LE CATEAU	14		The Battalion moved to LE CATEAU	App. 10. J.P.13.
"	15		Company training	J.P.13.
"	16		Parade Church service	J.P.13.
"	17		The Battalion went on a route march. Route BAZUEL – POMMEREUIL – FOREST – MONTAY.	App. 11. J.P.13.
"	18		All Coys on training	J.P.13.
"	19		A & B Coys on salvaging parties, C & D Coys on training. Reinforcement 16 Officers	J.P.13.
"	20		Same as for 19th.	J.P.13.
"	21		A & B Coys on training – C & D Coys on salvaging parties. 11 men returned from Hospital	J.P.13.
"	22		Same as for 21st.	J.P.13.

WAR DIARY
or
INTELLIGENCE SUMMARY.
(Erase heading not required.)

Army Form C. 2118.

1/8th Bn. The Worcestershire Regt.

Place	Date	Hour	Summary of Events and Information	Remarks and references to Appendices
	1918 Nov.			
LE CATEAU	23		Church Parade	
"	24		C & D Coys. Route march. A & B Coy working parties. 2 Officer Reinforcements	J.P.B.
"	25		A & B Coy working parties. C & D Coy training	J.P.B.
"	26		Same as for 25th	J.P.B.
"	27		As for 25th	J.P.B.
"	28		A & B Coy training. C & D Coy working parties. One Officer reinforcement	J.P.B.
CARNIERES	29		The Battalion marched to CARNIERES	Apx. B.
"	30		Inspections and cleaning and improvement of billets	J.P.B.

Commanding 1/8th Bn. Worcestershire Regt.

18th Bn. The Worcestershire Regt.

SECRET   Operation Order 102   Copy no.
VILLERS FAUX 1/100,000   less Hdqrs 8/11/18

Intention 1.   The Battalion will march to
ST BENIN tomorrow to watch a
demonstration on the use of Rifle

Instructions 2.
a/ Starting Point. Junction of BASUEL
+ LE CATEAU roads (near POMMEREUIL
church)
b/ Time 1300
c/ Order of Coys D C B Coy A Coy Hqts.
d/ Dress Fighting order. Haversack
on back.
e/ Formation 100ᵡ between platoons
f/ Haversack rations will be
carried. Dinners before starting
g/ A Coy will send 2 NCOs per
platoon.

Reports 3 To head of column

Distribution
1 + 4 Coys   S.H. Watkinson
5 File   Capt.
                    18th Bn. The Worcestershire Regt.

Secret.   1/8th Bn The Worcestershire Regt.   ② Copy No 1.
Ref 57A.N.W.   Instructions No 1.   2/11/18.
1/20,000

(1) The following instructions are a résumé of points gone over at recent C.Os. conferences, with the addition of such information as has been received since the last conference.

(2) On Zero day the 75th Brigade will cross the SAMBRE CANAL & establish a bridge head on the high ground east of LANDRECIES. The 50th Division is attacking on the left (149th Brigade on the right) & the 32nd Division on the right (96th Brigade on the left). The 74th Brigade will go through the 75th Brigade at Z+7 hours & the 7th Brigade is in Divisional Reserve.

(3) The 1/8th Royal Warwicks (left) + the 1/5th Gloucester Regt (right) will carry on the attack as far as the canal, arranging crossings on rafts N.W. & S.W. of LANDRECIES respectively, & pushing over small covering parties. The 1/8th Worcesters will cross the Canal & occupy the Red Line, (tracing being passed round) establishing an outpost line on the dotted red line; when they have been reinforced in the Red Line with a Company of Gloucesters & of Warwicks.

(4) At dusk on Y/Z night the 1/8th Worcesters will move up to MALGARNI, halting in the fields N.W. of that village. Coys will move from there so that they are in the following positions (shewn on trace) by Z-2 hours.

"A" Coy   Green lane from G.14.c.3.4 to G.14.c.8.7.
"B" "   On road from G.14.a.2.1 to G.14.a.8.1.
"C" "   On lane N. of LEFAUX from G.14.a.5.9 to G.8.c.9.0.
"D" "   On road from G.14.c.4.2 to G.20.a.8.7.
Bn H.Q. House G.13.d.8.1.

Lewis Gun Limbers will accompany battalion to junction of MALGARNI road + New Track (about G.19.a.5.9). "C" Coy limber will carry on as far as O.C. Coy wishes, & will then return to G.19.a.5.9. Tool limber + T.M. limber will bring up clothing, food, & rum. S.A.A. & Signals mules will accompany Bn H.Q., & stay in a field about G.19.b.6.9. As soon as the red line is gained, mules will take ammunition up to "A" Coy (O.C. "A" Coy will send back a guide), & dump it. On return they will be used to carry up clothes, food, & rum from the limbers.

(5) At Z+4 hours Coys will commence the advance in rear of the Gloucesters + Warwicks, who should be allowed to gain at least 400 yards (N.B. Coys - on - road). The barrage goes at 100 yards in 6 minutes. "C" + "D" Coys will move down the roads they are on towards

Instructions (Contd)

LANDRECIES. "A" Coy, with "B" Coy in touch in rear by connecting files, will move up to road Δ le in G14C, & strike across country, Bearing 112° true. Before Zero O.C. "D" Coy will get in touch with his 20 rafts at their assembly point, & later at their forming up point, & see that when the advance is commenced they follow his company.

(6) The crossing of the SAMBRE CANAL:
"D" Coy cross stream in G22 a & b on Gloucester rafts, & canal on their own as well.
"C" Coy cross on Warwick rafts.
"A" & "B" Coys cross either on main town bridge, if not blown up, or bridges over locks, if Sappers, who advance with Gloucesters, have made them; or failing this on rafts of first Coy across.

(7) When across "C" & "D" Coys go straight for their objectives on the red line (Boundaries. "D" Coy from G 23 c 0.2. to road junction G 23 d 3.8 inclusive; "C" Coy road junction to Canal at G17 b 7.0)
"A" Coy will mop up town & form an inner line of defence on its eastern outskirts.
"B" Coy will settle down in practice trenches about G 23 c 3.8 until the Warwicks & Gloucesters are up, when they will go forward & make good the outpost (dotted red) line. Each Coy will have two platoons in the line & one in support.

(8) Artillery. On Divisional Front. Four Brigades Field Artillery, One Brigade of Heavies, & some Corps Heavies. Barrage creeps at 100 yards in 6 minutes, starting from AB on trace at Z+4 hours, halting on CD (300 yards E. of Canal) from Z+3 hours 18 minutes to Z+4 hours 18 minutes, then carrying on to EF, where it forms a protective barrage for consolidation of Red Line, carrying on at Z+5½ hours for advance to Outpost Line.

(9) Machine Guns. At Zero barrage selected targets (48 guns). During crossing of canal 8 guns take up commanding positions in houses & railway cutting, engaging any target which appears. Also protect troops crossing, from counter attack. "B" Coy 25th M.G.C. less 1 Sn help in consolidating Red Line, with one gun on each flank & one in the centre.

10. <u>Tanks</u> will assist leading battalions to canal
 & then cruise about railway to assist crossing.
11. <u>R.A.F.</u> Keep a smoke cloud on high ground E. of
 LANDRECIES (enclosed by 160 contour) while
 crossing is going on. Call for flares at Z+5 hrs
 & Z+6 hours from Red Line. Counter attack
 patrols will indicate counter attacks by dropping
 a white parachute right over enemy centre.

Distribution
1 C.O.
2-5 Coys
6 Q.M.
7 T.O.
8 R.S.M.
9 File
10 War Diary

G.H. Watkinson
Capt. & Adjt.
1/8th Bn. The Worcestershire Regt.

SECRET.
Copy No. 11.

1/8th Bn. The Worcestershire Regt.
Operation Order No. 103.

Ref:- 57A. N.W.
FOREST 1/20,000.

Nov. 3rd 1918.

1. INTENTION.

The Battalion will move forward to Assembly Position tonight.

2. INSTRUCTIONS.

(a) Starting Point: Junction of BASUEL and LE CATEAU roads.
   Time: 2200.
   Dress: As detailed to Company Commanders.
   Order of Companies: 'C' 'A' 'B' 'D' H.Qrs.
   Formation: 100 yards between platoons.

(b) Lewis Gun Limbers will follow their Coys. Pack animals follow Bn. HQrs. T.M. Limbers will follow 'A' Coy.

(c) Guides for 'A', 'B', 'D' and Bn. H.Qrs. will be at L.24.a.4.8. in charge of 2/Lieut. E.F. BLACKLER. If the road is heavily shelled they will meet Battalion earlier and guide by an alternative route.

(d) Officers valises at Q.M's. Stores by 1800. Packs and blankets left outside each Company H.Q. under guard before moving off.

(e) Men dumped will report to R.S.M. H. Heath for orders tomorrow morning at 0900.

(f) Each C.Q.M.S. will go with his Company so that he will know place where cookers will be brought for tea at 0230 tomorrow.

(g) Coys will arrange for men to have soup before moving off tonight.

3. REPORTS.

(1) When Companies are in Assembly Position to L.24.a.4.8.
(2) When Companies are in Forming Up Position to House at G.13.d.9.1.

G.H. Watkinson
Capt. & A/Adjt.
1/8th Bn. The Worcestershire Regt.

Distribution:
Copy. No. 1. C.O.
" 2-6. Coys.
" 7. T.O.
" 8. Q.M.
" 9. R.S.M.
" 10 File
" 11 War Diary
" 12. M.O.

SECRET.   Copy No. 6

1/8 Bn. The Worcestershire Regt
Operations Order No 104
                                          Nov. 3. 1918

1. INTENTION.   LANDRECIES
        The Battalion will attack tomorrow
morning.

2. INSTRUCTIONS.
        (a) Zero: 0615
        (b) Objectives; Boundaries &c. as detailed
in Instructions 1 & Amendments.
        (c) The Right Flank Brigade will
attack at 05.45.

3. REPORTS.
        Bn. H.Q at house G.13.d.8.0 moving
forward by bounds along road running
Shrines G.20 through G.21 a & b on to
LANDRECIES. A Sentry will stop all
runners passing Bn. H.Q.

                                    J.W. Atkinson
                                    Capt & A/Adjt
                                    1/8 Bn. The Worcestershire Regt.

DISTRIBUTION
No 1- 4 Coys
    5 File
Issued to Coy. Cmdrs
    at 23.15

1/8th Bn. The Worcestershire Regt.

Died Lt C.N BARBER M.C

Of 19 Officers reported wounded, 2 died of wds
Lieut T.L JONES, 2/Lt C BROWN.
Of 405. O.R reported wounded, 17 died of wounds

Casualties for period 5.10.18 – 4.11.18.

<u>Officers</u>   Killed in Action.   3.
    Capt. H.G.C. CARTER M.C.
    2/Lt. M.D. KING.
    2/Lt. C A. CONNOR.
       WOUNDED. 19.

Lt. T.L. JONES. M.C.	2/Lt. L. GOODYEAR.
" R.J.C.V. HAWTREY.	Capt. G. H SMITH M.C.
Capt. G.A. MOORE. M.C. (RAMC)	Lt. W.S. GUNDRY. M.C.
Lt. F.W. WILES.	2/Lt. F.H. ASTILL.
2/Lt. G. HALES.	2/Lt. C. BROWN.
Lt. A.R. WATSON.	Lt. W.H. REYNOLDS.
Lt. R.S. MILLER.	2/Lt. J.H. GREENAWAY.
Lt. E. STAINTON.	Capt. J.O. WALFORD.
Capt. L.R. BAMFORD. M.C.	2/Lt. E. WEDGBURY. DCM. MM.
2/Lt. D. FRANKS. (7th Warwicks)	

    WOUNDED AT DUTY.   1.
2/Lt. S.T. BATEMAN. M.M
Other Ranks.
   Killed in Action   59.
   WOUNDED.   405.

1/8th Bn The Worcestershire Regiment.
Narrative of Operations 4th Nov 1918.

Ref 57A. N.W. 1/20000

(1)

(1) The 75th Infantry Brigade having been ordered to capture LANDRECIES, & to establish a bridge-head over the SAMBRE-OISE CANAL, the 1/5th Gloucester Regt. & the 1/8th Royal Warwick Regt. were detailed to make good the ground up to the CANAL, & to secure the crossing thereof; & the 1/8th Worcester Regt. to capture the town, & take up a line to the E, S.E., & S.

(2) The battalion formed up behind the Gloucesters & Warwicks in G14 at 0420 on 4.11.18. "D" Coy, right, "A" Coy, centre, "C" Coy, left, "B", reserve.

(3) The canal being 53 feet wide & 6 feet 6 ins deep, and it being anticipated that the enemy would blow up the bridges, the C.R.E. had constructed 80 rafts, each capable of supporting one man. Parties of R.E. & men of the Pioneer Bn. were detailed to carry the rafts to the canal, & by means of ropes affixed to each end, to ferry the infantry across, the raft in the first instance being paddled across by a sapper.

(4) Our barrage opened at 0615 hours, & the leading battalion moved forward. There was a thick ground-mist, & we had to move close behind them in order to keep touch.

(5) At 0624 hours O.C. "D" Coy (2nd Lt WEDGBURY D.C.M, M.M.) was wounded by one of our M.G. bullets, & 2nd Lt COLEMAN took over command of the Coy. Immediately after the advance commenced, the enemy artillery opened, firing at short range from just over the CANAL. After crossing the light railway in G21b, hostile M.G. fire was also encountered; but "D" Coy made rapidly for the foot-bridge over the stream at G22 a 44 secured it before the enemy could explode the mine, which was laid under the bridge. Owing to "D" Coy's rapid advance the Gloucesters & our own raft parties had been left behind, so a patrol was sent forward to the CANAL, & found foot-bridge at G22 d 05 still intact. "D" Coy therefore moved forward to the CANAL under heavy M.G. fire, but having now caught up our barrage, & by skilful use of L.G. covering fire, they crossed the CANAL & formed up on the other side at 0950 hours. "A" Coy of the Gloucesters then crossed over & formed up behind "D" Coy. At 1033 hours "D" Coy moved on again behind our barrage, meeting with little enemy resistance

The enemy had a strong post in a house, & a battery near by at G22 d 75, but they were captured (2 officers & 50 other ranks) before they could man their weapons.

(2)

(5) Cont:
The Objective was reached at 1115 hours & consolidated

(6) The Centre Coy ("A") under Capt Bomford. M.C., moved forward at 0615 hours, followed by the Reserve Coy ("B") under 2/Lt. BULLOCK. M.C., moving on a T.B. of 112°. The Gloucesters were held up at the light railway in G15d, by M.G. fire from a chateau at G.16a.11. "A" Coy pushed a platoon through the Gloucesters to attack this, & with the assistance of a Tank, & the support of the other two Platoons, it was captured together with 4 officers & 35 men. "A" Coy then moved forward again to G.16c.68, but had lost our barrage owing to the delay. Capt BOMFORD went on with a patrol to reconnoitre the bridge at G.23a.28, which was found to be intact. He sent back for the Coy, but in the meantime the enemy blew up the bridge. A platoon was then sent to the right to cross over behind "D" Coy, but they were met by concentrated M.G. fire, & held up. The R.E. party with two light bridges was then brought forward, & under the covering fire of the other two platoons these were placed across the lock at G.23a.17, & these two Platoons crossed over at 1245 hours, & pushed forward into LANDRECIES, leaving a guard on the crossing. "B" Coy then crossed over in support. "A" & "B" Coys then proceeded to mop up the town, being met by heavy fire from two batteries just to the S.E. & a few M.Gs in the town. The latter were captured, & then strong patrols of "B" Coy then pushed out & captured the two batteries & 46 prisoners. Capt BOMFORD was wounded about this time & 2/Lt BULLOCK took command of the two Companies & consolidated the objective.

(7) "C" (left) Coy moved forward behind the Warwicks at 0615 hours. They soon came in contact with enemy M.G. posts, of which they captured four (6 killed, 10 prisoners). Touch was lost with the Warwicks in the mist, & "C" Coy pushing on too quickly, suffered some casualties from our own barrage. Another M.G. was encountered at G.9d.50 (the team was killed & the gun captured).

(3)

(7) Cont'd. The advance was continued to the road at G16b07, where M.Gs. firing up the road from the railway, were met with, & mopped up with the aid of a Tank. The Coy then moved on against heavy artillery & M.G. fire, across the railway line, passing through the Warwicks, & reached the CANAL about G17d04. Here the enemy field guns, firing from just across the CANAL, were silenced by L.G. fire, the Raft parties were for brought forward, & our men were ferried over as described in para 3. This was done under enemy M.G. fire from a high building in LANDRECIES, but our covering fire made the enemy shooting ineffective. As soon as the Coy. was across (1045 hours) the advance was continued, against desultory M.G. fire, & the hospital at G23a82 was captured with 5 officers, & 40 men, 3 ambulances, 2 limbers, & 6 horses. The objective was then gained, & consolidation begun. Capt WALFORD was wounded about this time.

(8) The 11th Sherwood Foresters (74th Brigade) having passed through & occupied the Outpost Line in front, I reorganised on the Red Line, as shewn on the attached map.

(9) Captures.

	Prisoners		Guns	M.Gs.	Horses.
	Off	O.R.			
"A" Coy	4	70	2	25	12
"B" Coy		50	6		10
"C" Coy	5	45		6	6
"D" Coy	4	70	6	6	
	13	235	14	37	28

Also 3 motors & 2 horse ambulances, 2 limbers, dump of tools & large quantities of hospital equipment.

(10) Casualties

	Officers Wd'd.	Other Ranks	
		Killed	Wounded
"A" Coy	1	1	12
"B"	-	1	2
"C"	2	1	41
"D"	1	1	6
	4	4	61

6/11/18

SECRET 1/8 Bn. The Worcestershire Regt. Copy No...6...
         Operation Order No. 105

                                                5/11/18
1. INFORMATION.
     The advance is being continued to the Green line tomorrow
by the 74th Brigade. In the event of the 32nd Division not
coming up the 75th Brigade will be required to form a
defensive flank to the 74th Brigade.

2. INTENTION.
     The Battalion will move along the MAROILLES road
500x in rear of the 1/8 Warwicks Regt., if necessary forming
a defensive flank facing South East.

3. INSTRUCTIONS.
    (a) Coys will be ready to move off under cover at 0700
    (b) Order of Coys: B. A. C. D.
    (c) Formation:- 100 yards between Platoons leaving road
        at discretion of Platoon Comdrs. if shelling is heavy
    (d) O.C. "B" Coy will be responsible for chipping in
        after Warwicks at right distance (500 yards)
    (e) Lifebelts will be stacked outside Coy Hdqtrs before
        moving off.
    (f) The method of forming defensive flank will be as
        follows: Each Coy in turn will take up an outpost
        line facing right on a front of 500x. The 1/8 R. Warwicks
        being responsible for the first 2000x, "B" Coy next 500x
        and so on.

4. REPORTS.
     Bn. Hdqtrs. will open at 0830 at about G.23.d.6.3.
     Coys will send in Reports of progress every hour.

Acknowledge.   J.L. Watkinson

                                              Capt & Adjt
                                              1/8 Bn. The Worcestershire Regt.

Distribution
Nos 1-4. Coys

SECRET

Copy No 6
⑦

1/8. Bn the Worcestershire Regt
Operation Order No 106

Nov. 5. 1918

1. INFORMATION.

The 3nd Division having come up on our right flank the necessity for defending this flank has ceased.

2. INTENTION

The advance will be continued behind the 1/8 Warwicks.

3. INSTRUCTIONS.

(a) "B" and "A" Coys will be Vanguard. "B" company pushing forward patrols to keep in touch with the situation forward. "A" Coy. finding a 1 platoon flank guard to the Battalion in case we get forward of the 32nd Div's advanced troops again.

(b) "C" & "D" Coys will move in columns of route 300° in rear of the VanGuard. They will be Main guard.

4. REPORTS.

To rear of Main Guard.

J.h. Watkinson

Distribution
No 1-4. Coys
 " 5 Retained

10.12 hours.

Capt & a/adjt
1/8 Bn. Worcs. Regt

SECRET   Copy No. 6

1/8 Bn. Worcestershire Regt.
Operation Order No. 107

Ref. Sheet 57A.NW.   7/11/18

1 INFORMATION

The 7th & 74th Brigade will continue the advance today. The 75th Bde will march in rear.

2 INTENTION

The Battalion will continue the march in rear of the 1/8 Warwicks.

3 INSTRUCTIONS

(a) TIME. At half an hour's notice after 0900

(b) ORDER B.A. H.Q. C.D.   O.C. "B" Coy responsible for connection with Warwicks

(c) DRESS Full Marching Order with packs.

(d) ROUTE MAROILLES – TAISNIERES – DOMPIERRE

(e) FORMATION 200x between Coys. 500x between Btns.

(f) Limbers in rear of Coys. T.M. limbers in rear of Bn H.Q.

(g) Lewis guns & ammunition to be loaded under Coy arrangements at once. The guns will not be put into chest but kept in bags on top of ammunition. Cookers will be left behind.

4 REPORTS To Bn. H.Q in centre of column.

Distribution   J. [illegible] Capt & Adjt
No 1–4 Coys   1/8 Bn. Worc. Regt
    5 Retained

SECRET   Copy No. 6

1/8 Bn. Worcestershire Regt
Operation Order No. 108

Ref. 57A
                                          9
                                          8/11/18
1. INFORMATION
    The Brigade is moving to PREUX where it will be billetted.

2. INTENTION
    The Bn is marching to PREUX today

3. INSTRUCTIONS
   (a) Starting point "C" Coy Billet
   (b) Time 0915. Order D.C. H.Q. A.B.
       Dress: Marching Order & Shrapnel helmets
       Formation: 100ˣ between Coys. 50ˣ between each 12 vehicles. Route MAROILLES – LANDRECIES – Cross Roads A 20 C.4.1
   (c) Baggage. Officers valises at Stores by 0730. Mess boxes outside Bn H.Q. 0845
   (d) Dinners on March, ready 1150
   (e) Transport. L.G. Limbers with Coys. remainder in rear of Batln.

4. REPORTS
    To Head of Columns.

Distribution
1. C. Coy
2. A & B Coy
3. D Coy
4. QM & T.O.   5 retained

                                J.W. Atkinson
                                Capt & Adjt
                                1/8 Bn Worc Regt

1/8 Bn. The Worcestershire Regt.

SECRET   Operation Order No 109   Copy No 9

Ref: 57 b N.E. }
     57 a N.W. } 1/20000   13.11.1918

1. **Information.** The Brigade is moving to LE CATEAU to day.
2. **Intention.** The Battalion will march to LE CATEAU to day.
3. **Instructions**
   (a) Starting Point PREUX Church
   (b) Time 1020
   (c) Order. Drums B. A. HQ. C.D. Transport.
   (d) Dress. Marching Order. Shrapnel helmets on Packs
   (e) Formation 500^x between Battns. 100^x between Coys. 25^x between each group of Six Vehicles.
   (f) Route Cross Roads A 20 c 4.1 - ROBERSART - LES GRANDS CHENES - FONTAINE AU BOIS - FME DES TILLEULS LE CORDEAU.
   (g) Transport. L.G limbers with Coy. Sgt Pitt to see Guns loaded, 2 Men per team report Transport 0830
   (h) Baggage. Blankets in bundles of 10 stacked at Stores by 0800. Officers valises & mess boxes (less green box) at stores by 0845. Mess Cart will call for Green boxes at 0915.
   (i) Billet inspection 0930
   (j) Billetting party 4 Chevaliers & 2/Lt BATEMAN M.M. Report at 54 Bde HQ at LE CATEAU.
4. **Reports** To Head of Column

Issued at 6 a.m by Runner

Distribution   Sd/ G.L. WATKINSON
Normal   Capt & A/adjt
                      1/8 Worcestershire Regt

SECRET

1/8 Bn. The Worcestershire Regt
Operation Order No 110.

Copy No 9

Ref: VALENCIENNES
1/100.000

Nov. 17. 1918.

1. **INTENTION.**
The Battn will carry out a route march to-morrow.

2. **INSTRUCTIONS.**
    (a) <u>Starting Point</u>. Broken Railway bridge over BASUEL road.
    (b) <u>Time</u>: 0915
    (c) <u>Order</u>: Drums C. D. H.Q. B. A. Transport.
    (d) <u>Dress</u>: Marching Order.
    (e) <u>Route</u>: BASUEL - POMMEREUIL - FOREST - MONTAY.
    (f) <u>Lewis Gun</u> limbers will follow their Coys. Two men per team will report to Transport 0815 to load limbers under supervision of Sgt Raby.
    (g) <u>Pack Mules</u> will march in rear of the Battalion

3. **REPORTS.**
To head of Column.

G. H. Watkinson.
Capt & A/Adjt
1/8 Bn. The Worcestershire Regt.

Distribution:-
Copy No 1. C.O.
    " 2-6 Coys
    " 7 T.O.
    " 8 War Diary
    " 9 File

SECRET.

1/8th Bn The Worcestershire Regiment.
Operation Order No. 111.

⑫   Copy No. 11

Ref:- 57 B. N.E. 1/20,000.
57 B. 1/40,000.

Nov. 28th 1918.

INFORMATION. 1.
The 75th Brigade group will move to CARNIERES area to-morrow.

INTENTION. 2.
The Battalion will march to CARNIERES to-morrow.

DETAIL. 3.

(a) Starting Point. Cross roads near "A" Coy billet. K34d 9560 (Sheet 57 B.N.E)
(b) Time. 1105.
(c) Order of March. B, A, HQ, D, C, Transport.
(d) Dress.
(e) Formation. { Marching Order. Shrapnel helmets on back of packs.
                 { Jerkins if worn must be underneath jackets.
100 yards between Coys., & 50 yards between each group of six vehicles. Distances to be gained after starting point.

(f) Route.
Road junction K34a 00. INCHY, BEAUVOIS, ENCAMBRESIS, Road junction G25d 10 (Ref 57B 1/40,000).

(g) Lewis Gun Limbers.
Will follow in rear of their Coys.

(h) Baggage.
Blankets (tightly rolled in bundles of 10, tied at both ends & in the middle) will be stacked at Q.M. Stores 0645.
Officers' Valises & Mess Boxes at Q.M. Stores 0930.
Mess Cart will call for Green Boxes at 1000.

(i) Unless the weather is unsuitable there will be a halt for dinners from 1250 to 1350. Separate instructions have been issued by Second in Command with regard to this.

REPORTS. 4.
To head of column.

G. L. Watkinson
Capt & A/Adjt.
1/8th Bn The Worcestershire Regiment.

Distribution.
No. 1. C.O.
2-6 Coys
7 T.O.
8 Q.M.
9 R.S.M.
10 File
11 War Diary
12 M.O.

CONFIDENTIAL.

25th Division, "G".

        Enclosed please find WAR DIARIES for November 1918 for the following:-

    75th Inf. Bde (in duplicate) together with copies of Bde
            Orders, Instructions and Narrative.

    1/8th R.Warwick Regt.

    1/5th Gloucester Regt.

    1/8th Worcester Regt together with Battn Orders and
            Instructions, and Narrative.

14.11.1918.   Brigadier General.
                                  Comdg., 75th Infantry Brigade.

HEADQUARTERS
75th INFANTRY BRIGADE
B.M.X.432.

WAR DIARY
or
INTELLIGENCE SUMMARY.
(Erase heading not required.)

Army Form C. 2118.

1/8th Bn. The Worcestershire Regt.

Vol 4 5

Place	Date 1918 Dec.	Hour	Summary of Events and Information	Remarks and references to Appendices
CARNIERES	1		Voluntary church service	
"	2		A & B Coys less Specialist classes at disposal of Coy C.O.s for training. Specialist classes held in Lewis gun, Signalling, Stretcher Bearing work, and Educational Classes for young A & B, and Shortland. C & D Coys provided cleaning up parties.	
"	3		As for 2nd Dec.	
"	4		The C.O. inspected A & B Coys. The Battalion was turned up to see this hardly its King George V in the afternoon.	
"	5		The C.O. inspected C & D Coys & its details. A & B Coys on ackworks.	
"	6		The Battalion marched to AVESNES for Baths.	
"	7		A & B Coys on ackworks. C & D Coys on training. Received Educational scheme was held. The Divisional General presented medal ribbons to Officers & men of the battalion in the presence of representative parties of the units of the Brigade.	
"	8		Parade Church Service.	
"	9		A & B Coys on training. C & D Coys on ackworks & Educational	

Army Form C. 2118.

WAR DIARY
or
INTELLIGENCE SUMMARY.

1/8th Bn. The Worcestershire Regt.

(Erase heading not required.)

Place	Date 1918 Dec.	Hour	Summary of Events and Information	Remarks and references to Appendices
CARRIERES	9		Steinlet Classes were held. The Divisional Commander made	
	10		further presentation of medal ribbons. A & B Coys Training. Special & Educational Classes, C & D Coy on salvage work.	
"	11		Battalion Parade for Ceremonial Drill.	
"	12		All Coys on salvage work. Classes as usual.	
"	13		As for 12th.	
"	14		As for the 11th.	
"	15		Parade Church Service. The first men in the battalion to be demobilised were dispatched to CAMBRAI (2 men — 2 young miners)	
CAMBRAI	16		The Battalion moved to CAMBRAI (Sunday)	
"	17		Coys at disposal of Coy. Cmdr. for inspection and the cleaning up of billets.	
"	18		Coys. at disposal of Cmdr. for training. The Co. inspected billets	
"	19		All Coys. worked on salvage area. Educational classes & Steinlet classes as usual. Brigade Classes in French Bookkeeping & Machine Drawing met.	

Army Form C. 2118.

WAR DIARY
or
INTELLIGENCE SUMMARY
(Erase heading not required.)

1/8th Bn. The Worcestershire Regt.

Place	Date 1918 Dec.	Hour	Summary of Events and Information	Remarks and references to Appendices
CAMBRAI	20		Battalion Parade for Ceremonial drill, Specialist & Educational classes.	Hyle
"	21		Battalion Parade for Ceremonial drill. Classes as usual.	Hyle
"	22		Voluntary Church Service	Hyle
"	23		All Coys (two classes) on Salvage work.	Hyle
"	24		The Battalion had Bath.	Hyle
"	25		Church Parade. Service. The men had their Xmas Dinner in the evening.	Hyle
"	26		In training for Salvage. Prize Sports were held for Wrestley & Westwisleth & the Feat River	Hyle
"	27		All Coys (two classes) on Salvage	Hyle
"	28		Battalion Parade for ceremonial drill. Rehearsal of Trooping the Colour	Hyle
"	29		Voluntary Church Service	Hyle
"	30		On 1st 28th inst.	Hyle
"	31		All Coys on Salvage work. A party was sent to witness the Trophy of the Colours of 1st/8 Royal Warwickshire Regt.	Hyle

Reinforcements
2/Lieut 8 Dec 8 & Lieut C.L. de C. HINDS
" 12 8 O.R.
" 17 6 O.R.
" 16 244 H.C. STARR and 2/Lt A.E. HAMMOND
" 31 69/1 T. STINTON

H.T. Clarke
Lieut. Col.
Commanding 1/8th Bn. The Worcestershire Regt.

WAR DIARY
INTELLIGENCE SUMMARY

Army Form C. 2118.

1/8th Bn. The Worcestershire Regt.

Vol 46

Place	Date	Hour	Summary of Events and Information	Remarks and references to Appendices
CAMBRAI	1919 Jan 1st		Battalion Parade (Practice Trooping the Colours) 10 OR Demobilized.	A.H.16
"	2nd		Battalion Parade (Trooping the Colours) One OR Demobilized.	A.H.16
"	3rd		All Coys one hour Recreational Training. Baths & Education Classes	A.H.16
"	4th		All Coys worked on Salvage Areas. Specialist Classes (Lewis Gun and Signalling) Education Classes. One OR & One OR demobilized	A.H.16
"	5th		Voluntary Church Services	A.H.16
"	6th		All Coys worked on Salvage Areas Specialist Classes (Lewis Gun Signalling) Education Classes	A.H.16
"	7th		All Coys on Salvage Specialist Classes (Lewis Gun & Signalling) Education Classes	A.H.16
"	8th		Battalion Parade (Route March)	A.H.16
"	9th		All Coys on Salvage Specialist Classes (Lewis Gun & Signalling) Education Classes	A.H.16
"	10th		All Coys on Salvage Lewis Gun Signalling and Education Classes	A.H.16
"	11th		Coys at the Disposal of Coy Cmdrs for Training	A.H.16
"	12th		Parade Church Services	A.H.16

WAR DIARY
INTELLIGENCE SUMMARY.

1/8th Bn. The Worcestershire Regt

Army Form C. 2118.

(Erase heading not required.)

Place	Date	Hour	Summary of Events and Information	Remarks and references to Appendices
CAMBRAI	Jan 13		All Coys One and a half hours training. Baths, 1 Or and P.O.R. demobilized	H.J.C.
	14th		All Coys Salvage. Lewis Gun Signalling and Education Classes held	H.J.C.
	15th		"B" "C" and "D" Coys at disposal of Coy Cmdr for training	
			"A" Coy Salvage. Lewis Gun Signalling and Education Classes	H.J.C.
			Three O.R. Demobilized	
	16th		All Coys Salvage. Lewis Gun Signalling and Education Classes held	H.J.C.
	17th		All Coys Salvage. Lewis Gun Signalling and Education Classes	H.J.C.
	18th		All Coys at disposal of Coy Commanders for training	
			Eight O.R. demobilized	H.J.C.
	19th		Voluntary Church Services. Five O.R. demobilized	H.J.C.
	20th		C and D Coys did one hour's training. A and B Coys Education	
			Battalion marched to Baths. One Officer and Seven O.R. demobilized	H.J.C.
	21st		C and D Coys One hour's training and Education. A and B Coys worked on Salvage Area. Signalling Class held. Eight O.R. demobilized.	H.J.C.
	22nd		"A" and "B" Coys One hour's training, and two hours Education. C and D Coys Salvage work. Battalion Res 360 O.R. on Education Classes. One Officer and 10 O.R. demobilized	H.J.C.

Army Form C. 2118.

WAR DIARY
or
INTELLIGENCE SUMMARY.

1/8th Bn. The Worcestershire Regt.

(Erase heading not required.)

Place	Date	Hour	Summary of Events and Information	Remarks and references to Appendices
CAMBRAI	1919 Jan 23rd		"A" and "B" Coys one hours training, two hours Education, "C" and "D" Coys worked on Salvage Areas.	H.Y.6.
	24th		"A" and "B" Coys worked on Salvage area, "C" and "D" Coy training and Education.	H.Y.6.
	25		"A" and "B" Coy training and Education, "C" and "D" Coys Salvage. Eight O.R. demobilized.	H.Y.6.
	26		Parade Church Services. 1 Officer and eleven OR demobilized.	H.Y.6.
	27		"C" and "D" Salvage Work. "A" and "B" training and Education. Ten OR demobilized.	H.Y.6.
	28		"A" and "B" Coy Salvage Work, "C" and "D" Coys training and Education. Fifteen OR demobilized.	H.Y.6.
	29		"A" and "B" Coy training and Education, "C" and "D" Coys Salvage Work. 1 Officer and 12 OR demobilized.	H.Y.6.
	30		"A" and "B" Coy Salvage Work, "C" and "D" Coy training and Education, "C" and "D" Battalion Baths.	H.Y.6.
	31		"A" and "B" Coy Education, "C" and "D" on hours training.	H.Y.6.

H.Y.Clarke. Lieut. Col.
Commanding 1/8th Bn. The Worcestershire Regt.

1/8th Bn. The Worcestershire Regt.

Army Form C. 2118.

WAR DIARY
~~INTELLIGENCE SUMMARY.~~
(Erase heading not required.)

Vol 47

Place	Date	Hour	Summary of Events and Information	Remarks and references to Appendices
CAMBRAI	1919 May 1		"A" "B" Coys Salvage. C & D Coys vocational Training & Education.	17 O.R. Demobilized. A.F.B.
"	2		Voluntary Church Service.	16 O.R. " A.F.B.
"	3		A & B Coys. 1/2 day Training & Education. C & D Coys. Salvage work.	16 O.R. " (2/Lt ST. BATE (PW)) A.F.B.
"	4		C & D " " " " A & B " "	18 O.R. " A.F.B.
"	5		A & B " " " " C & D " "	" A.F.B.
"	6		A & B Coys. Training & Rections. C & D Coys. Education. Games.	A.F.B.
"	7		A & B Coys. 1/2 day Training. Education Games. C & D. " " Arrival of 6 Carreaton.	6 O.R. demobilized. A.F.B.
"	8		All Coys. Training & Education	16 O.R. " A.F.B.
"	9		Voluntary Church Services.	" A.F.B.
"	10		A & B Coys. Salvage work. C & D Coys. Training & Education	2/Lt P.W. Jewson 9,12. O.R. demobilized A.F.B.
"	11		A & B Coys. Training & Education. C & D Coys. Salvage work	14 O.N. demobilize A.F.B.
"	12		A & B Coys. Salvage work. C & D Coys. Training & Education	" A.F.B.
"	13		A & B " Training & Education. C & D Coys. Salvage work.	12 O.R. demobilized. A.F.B.
"	14		All Coys. Training & Education. Games & Paths	11 O.R. " A.F.B.
"	15		A & B Coys. Training & Education. C & D Coys. Salvage Work.	11 O.R. " A.F.B.
"	16		Voluntary Church Services	11 O.R. " A.F.B.

1/8th Bn. The Worcestershire Regt.

WAR DIARY
INTELLIGENCE SUMMARY
(Erase heading not required.)

Army Form C. 2118.

Place	Date	Hour	Summary of Events and Information	Remarks and references to Appendices
CAMBRAI	1919 Feb 17		A + B Coy. Salvage Work. C + D Coys. Training + Education. 12 O.R. Demobilized	H.I.C.
	18		A. Coy. Training + Education. B. Training + Bathing. C + D Coys. Salvage work.	H.I.C.
	19		A + B Coy. Salvage work. C + D. Coy. Training + Education	H.I.C.
	20		A + B. Training + Education. C + D Coys. Salvage work. 11 O.R. Demobilized	H.I.C.
	21		A + B Coy. Salvage. C + D Coys. Training + Education. 27 O.R. "	H.I.C.
	22		Battalion Parade. 34 O.R. "	H.I.C.
	23		Voluntary Church Services.	H.I.C.
	24		All Coys. Baths. C + D Coy. Education. 28 O.R. "	H.I.C.
	25		All Coys. on Salvage work. (The Battalion was formed into a draft of 200 men details owing to Demobilization are to a Draft of 200 men details. B. Coy. forming the draft Coy. and for duty with the 4th Foresters/Miner.) 7 O.R. "	
	26		A. Coy. Leaving the evening. Footnote. The Battalion 1st Dft Team that B. Coy. 2/Lt P. Warwicks - the 2nd Draft by 4 goes to 2.	H.I.C.
	27		Battalion Parade inspection of Clothing.	H.I.C.
	28		Training + Education	H.I.C.
			Battalion engaged on Salvage work. 5 O.R. Demobilized	H.I.C.

H.I.Clarke
Lieut. Col.
Commanding 1/8th Bn. The Worcestershire Regt.

www.ingramcontent.com/pod-product-compliance
Lightning Source LLC
Chambersburg PA
CBHW081444160426
43193CB00013B/2382